Reasoning from Scripture

with our

Baptist Brethren

A Handbook for the Paedobaptist Apologist

BY

Andrew W. Camp

Present Reign Publications
www.presentreignpublications.com

ISBN 978-1-945897-17-7

Reasoning from Scripture

with our

Baptist Brethren

A Handbook for the Paedobaptist Apologist

"The first one to plead his cause seems right, until his neighbor
comes and examines him."
(Proverbs 18:17)

BY

Andrew W. Camp

www.presentreignpublications.com

ISBN 978-1-945897-17-7

Printed by Present Reign Publications in the USA
2018

Dedication

To Joshua and Laura Ohlman, and all the little disciples of
Christ that come along due to your union, I lovingly
dedicate this book. May the Lord be pleased to add to the
"Church in your house."

CONTENTS

FOREWORD

God expects parents to raise their covenant children in the discipline and instruction of the Lord. Baptism is the God given sign and seal of our union with the family of God. If you could be part of any family on earth to which family would you belong? How would you decide? Position, privilege, or future? There is a family which has all of these and so much more, but its riches and glories are regularly underappreciated and under realized. The reality is, in this family there need be no dread of the future, no fear of dying, no despair in failure (because in this family — failure is not permanent). In this family the future continues to get brighter and brighter. God Himself is the Head of the family and administers its affairs.

One of the most significant events in our lives as Christian parents is the presentation of our children for the sacrament of baptism. While obedience to God's command is always the key to blessing, surely this blessing is enhanced by an understanding of what transpires in this glorious mystery.

As I stand before God with my child in my arms, I must ask myself, who am I and who is my child that we are here before the Church of Jesus Christ to receive the sign and seal of the eternal covenant. In Acts 2:39 I am told: "The promise is for you and your children." This is covenant language. God's promise to His people is called a covenant — Genesis 17:7. This is further confirmed in Galatians 3:29, "If you belong to Christ, then you are Abraham's offspring, heirs according to promise."

I have thought for a long time that the church needs a book like this one by Andrew Camp. It will surely meet a critical need. This whole concept of Federal headship is ignored by much of the church today. This is tragic, because failure to understand Federal headship is failure to understand much of God's revelation. I strongly urge the studying of this fine book by Andrew Camp.

Pastor Don Rackley, Evangel Presbyterian (PCA), Wichita KS

Preface

The purpose of this book is twofold. On the one hand, I wanted to make a go-to guide, or handbook, for those of the Paedobaptist persuasion that are not necessarily as studied in the subject as maybe they should be, or perhaps they genuinely don't have the time to be. To these, I hope this book can guide you in your conversations to lovingly engage with our Credobaptist brethren. Please note that this book is addressed from the very title to my "brethren," and brethren they are. I'm not so bitterly partisan that I will not rejoice in our common faith with those who happen to be in error on baptism. On the contrary, I love my brethren and wish them to have the same joy that I have in understanding this doctrine correctly. Nor do I think that this is such an important doctrine that we cannot worship together or partake of the Lord's Body and Blood together. But unfortunately, our Credobaptist brethren view this doctrine as so important that they will refuse membership in their churches unless you have been baptized as an adult by immersion. This is indeed unfortunate for those of us who do not live near a faithful Paedobaptist church. I have found myself unable to join a local church, because the only Reformed brethren within a two-hour drive were Baptists. These were churches that I would have been happy to put my membership in, but they would not have me. This is no small struggle.

On the other hand, I wish this to be a case for the Credobaptists themselves to challenge themselves with. Go ahead and work your way through the various arguments presented herein. I consider it a privilege to reason with you via writing, and I will yet consider it a greater privilege to reason further with you if you so wish. I am available for public debate.

"Religious controversy has its evils; but they are trifling compared to those which pertain to indifference to the truth. Error is the parent of division and sectarianism; and thorough, vigorous, persistent discussion is the only remedy for this evil, the only path to unity in truth. "Earnestly contend for the faith," is a Divine injunction. Truth never suffers in a fair contest. The strength of error is in concealment and quiet; hence it deprecates discussion, shuns the light.

Honest men love to state their doctrine, and urge their reasons, and have them assailed, tried, tested by vigorous combat. As they love truth more than victory, they are glad to see every fallacy exposed, every false position demolished, every error confuted, that they may not suffer the great misfortune of believing and defending a lie."[1]

I find myself in agreement with the above statement. The Church is suffering from those who do not wish to have "thorough, vigorous, persistent discussion" about this topic (or any topic, for that matter); and so we continue in the errors of our forefathers. I treasure the "combat" that honest Christian men can have when they are passionate about that truth. And that is precisely why I am no longer a Credobaptist. I have seen every fallacy of the Credobaptist position exposed, its every false position demolished, and every error confuted. Thus, I no longer believe nor defend the error of Credobaptism. I pray the same for all of my Credobaptist brethren who may read this book.

A more modern representative of the Credobaptist view says this:

"Some within the Christian confession claim that baptism should be classified as a minor issue. Such a sentiment is misdirected... Baptism is important precisely because it is tied to the gospel, to the saving work that Christ accomplished in his death and resurrection. We do not think baptizing infants is merely a

---

[1] G. H. Ball, Christian Baptism. The Duty, The Act, And the Subjects. 1860

iv

minor mistake, even though we rejoice in the evangelical credentials of many with whom we disagree."[1]

I echo his sentiments, except, of course, that baptizing infants is a mistake; and I hope that more Credobaptists will take up the challenge of really seeing what baptism is all about in the Bible. It's been a wonderful study for me, as I'm sure it will be for anyone that puts forward the effort to know what the Bible teaches on this subject. But having said that, the subject of baptism has produced such a vast amount of literature that the study of it all would require more time than an average human being has to spend; and so it doesn't usually get done. Indeed, just when I think I have a good grasp of what such-and-such a text means, I read another book from antiquity that sheds even more light on it. And so we should not be surprised when poor arguments for either position are used by would-be apologists for either position. We simply don't have time to spend years of our life studying a topic that many on both sides profess to be "secondary" to our faith. Admittedly, it's not like we're arguing about justification by faith or the doctrine of the Trinity; but the doctrine of baptism does happen to be a Biblical doctrine with no small amount of space devoted to it in the Bible. So it's definitely worth our time to examine it in more detail than most Christians do.

---

[1] Thomas R. Schreiner and Shawn D. Wright. Believers Baptism. 2006

V

INTRODUCTION

Out of the many books I have read on baptism, very few do not start out with the question: "So why on earth do we need another book on baptism?" I was tempted to start this book the same way. But I have also learned that acquired knowledge requires reformulations of that knowledge for a new generation. This book is just that—a reformulation of what the author sees as the best arguments passed down through history for the practice of Paedobaptism by effusion; along with a few newer arguments from the author's own storehouse of wisdom, which he has gleaned over the past 15 years or so of studying this issue. The modern books on baptism seem to be based on other modern books on baptism. I have seen very few that reference works older than this century. And yet the golden years of this debate were the 18ᵗʰ and 19ᵗʰ centuries. That is when this topic was debated in more than an intramural tone. Case in point: nobody from our era is writing four volumes on the meaning of the Greek word βαπτίζω.[1]

Why is it that every generation thinks they need to re-invent the wheel? I think the modern writers are not nearly as educated, erudite, or eloquent as those of the immediate post-Puritan era. In my view, the arguments used during those golden years were far more persuasive; and they are not even referenced today. If you were to read only modern books on the doctrine of the Trinity, you would be losing out on the rich history of the arguments that formulated our modern thinking on the topic. Well, the same is true for any doctrine. You want to read the new, but you cannot neglect the old. And my experience with the topic of baptism is that we tend to neglect the old.

I have numerous books on baptism sitting on my shelf that were written within the last 50 years or so, and not one of them references any of the books that I researched for this book older than this century. Now, to be sure, I am only restating the arguments that I

---

[1] James Dale did write 4 volumes on the meaning on this one word. And believe it or not, it makes for some very good reading. See it in the appendix.

have learned from my beloved brethren of the past, who are right now bowing before our Savior's throne and whose writings adorn the walls of my study. I am continually reminded how much I owe to my Savior for His gift to the Church of "pastors and teachers" who "equip the saints" for the work of ministry. By God's grace, I have many hundreds of volumes of this "equipment" that they have left behind; and I do not intend to neglect it.

That being said, this book is not just a compilation of those arguments. I have tried to synthesize them and restate them so as to make sense to the "sound-bite" sensibilities that we have grown up with in our culture. As a former Baptist, I know what I wanted to see presented as proof for the Paedobaptist position. I have tried to frame this in such a way, that it would have answered my objections and presented the positive proof I needed, in order to convince me.

While I have tried to present my arguments in logical order, you may find that they are more encyclopedic than one cohesive whole. If you are new to this debate, please start with Chapter 1 and get a good basis for the discussion. If you are an experienced Christian who wants to get to the heart of the arguments, then read Chapters 2 and 3 to get a good understanding of why the Paedobaptist position is right and the Credobaptist position is wrong; then use the rest of the book as an encyclopedia of arguments on what I term the *minutia* of the debate. Not all Credobaptists are going to need all of these arguments. Some just need to know what baptism actually is; and suddenly, they will understand the rest.

The layout of this book is simple. I tackle the main arguments first; then I dwell on the *minutia*. These are the various little details that arguments on baptism too often get caught up in. For many in the Credobaptist camp, they only need to be shown how their main arguments are not Biblical, and then they quickly start to think rightly. For others, you will need to disprove every jot and tittle of every single argument they have; and they still won't give it up. Those persons are married to their doctrine and will never divorce it, no matter what. If we had a text of Scripture that explicitly said, "Thou shalt baptize newborn babes!" we would still have these types of Credobaptists to deal with. They would tell us that the "newborn babes" are spoken of metaphorically because 1 Peter 2:2 speaks of adults as "newborn babes" in need of their milk..."the word." And since a literal "newborn babe" can't *read* "the word," then obviously, "Thou shalt baptize newborn babes" must be referring only to adults who can read. Think I'm exaggerating? Credobaptists have come up with arguments sillier than this, as you will see throughout this book!

You see, when someone reads the Bible with the understanding of "baptism" meaning to dunk a person's entire body in water; then when that person reads a verse like, "John came baptizing in the wilderness and preaching a baptism of repentance for the remission of sins" (Mark 1:4), he will undoubtedly see his view of baptism. But so will the person who understands baptism to be by sprinkling. The former sees John dunking thousands of persons in the Jordan River;[1] the latter sees John standing in or by the water, dipping a hyssop branch in the water and sprinkling the people as they come by or using some sort of vessel to pour the water over the persons. So much of the interpretation of these verses is purely *presuppositional*. Never mind that it would be impossible for one man to stand waist deep in the water, for fifteen hours a day, every day of the year, dunking thousands of persons. Never mind the obvious conclusions... presuppositions rule. So what do we do about that? We destroy the presuppositions. Once their thoughts are in turmoil, you can actually present a coherent view and they will, hopefully, cling to it.

And don't think that this mentality is only found in our Credobaptist brethren. Paedobaptists are often in the exact same frame of

---

[1] Wayne Grudem asserts, "The practice of baptism in the New Testament was carried out in one way: the person being baptized was immersed or put completely under the water and then brought back up again." Systematic Theology pg 967

In proof of that assertion, Mr. Grudem quotes the passage of Scripture where it says, "They put them under water and then brought them back up again"... or...well...maybe not. Actually, he does make the same assumptions which render the Scriptures unintelligible, and force us to believe impossibilities; like the Israelites carrying 200,000 bathtubs around the desert, or immersing themselves in their drinking water. See the section in Chapter 6 entitled The Self-Washings.

mind. As a matter of fact, Paedobaptists are perhaps worse in this regard, because they tend to be married to their confessions. I love the confessions; don't get me wrong. But let me just say that Paedobaptists tend to use the confessions in ways that contradict the very confessions they say they hold to. If I ask you what you believe, and you quote to me from a Creed or Confession, you have done nothing wrong. After all, that is what Creeds and Confessions are...statements of what those who hold to them *believe*. But if I ask you why you believe something, and you quote to me a Confession, then you are elevating the Confession to the level of Scripture—the very thing the Confessions warn against. Conservative Presbyterians and the Dutch Reformed seem to be the most susceptible to this error, although anyone can fall into it. Remember, Creeds and Confessions = what a person believes. The Bible = why we believe what we believe. Thus, I will not be using Creeds or Confessions in this book, except to point out what a particular tradition believes.

All right, before you read this book you need to know that there is a difference between a *sound* argument and a *persuasive* argument. An argument can be perfectly true and sound, and yet not be persuasive to those you are arguing with. There are many reasons that a sound argument will not necessarily *persuade*. The presuppositions of your opponent may be coloring how he views your argument; your presentation might not be persuasive; it might be ignorant; or it might be all of the above. When I was a Credobaptist, I was not persuaded by the arguments of Paedobaptists, largely because I was convinced that the Bible doesn't ever command infant baptism, and that you need to believe to be baptized...etc. I was quite honestly surprised when I was confronted with the *actual* arguments for Paedobaptism and against Credobaptism. But one of the problems I have encountered while trying to talk to my Credo brethren, is their sound-bite theology. They want "a verse." And Presbyterians are not used to arguing in that way. They are used to arguing in vast swaths of Biblical truth. They take you way up on a mountain and show you the entire Biblical story, and how it all fits together in the framework of the covenants. Undoubtedly, it is a beautiful picture; but it's also unpersuasive to a sound-bite mentality. They want to see a verse! I got bored reading the lengthy treatises that Paedobaptists write on this doctrine. However, I did eventually get up on that covenantal mountain and see these doctrines from way up there, but my brethren still see the arguments from way down here. They don't want to see how covenantal unity is traced all through the Scripture. They want to see a verse that tells them that infants should be baptized, and that by sprinkling. So it is the position of the Author that baptism is to be an administered rite, done by effusion, to all who are in a covenant relationship to Jesus Christ. All will be proven while we reason *from Scripture*.

There are so many Credobaptist persuasions, and I have tried to address them all; but for the most part, this book can be considered a rebuttal to the Reformed Credobaptist view. With this in mind, there will be some sections that do not apply in any way to the particular Credobaptist that you are reasoning with. A Reformed Credobaptist may not need to see the same proofs that an Arminian Credobaptist would need. So use this book to acquaint yourself with the different viewpoints, and be prepared to answer them. Please be aware that although I am dealing particularly with Reformed Baptists, I will be using the term Baptist and Credobaptist, in this book, to refer to all those who hold the view that personal faith and confession is an absolute prerequisite to being baptized. Both topics of the mode of baptism and the recipients of baptism are addressed throughout this book, as they are intimately intertwined.

I will briefly touch on Federal theology, which is just another name for Covenant theology. So a quick note on this will be proper. Covenant theology can be said to be a complete system of Biblical interpretation which combats the dispensational approach of interpretation, which much of the modern evangelical Church has adopted. But it began as an attempt to explain to Credobaptists why it was proper to baptize our children. I think it is a good and valid argument, and I fully embrace it as the most proper construct of theology. However, that is not the same as saying it's the best *argument* for Paedobaptism. If you read any of the Puritans' appeals to Genesis 17, or more modern books like Pierre Marcel's *The*

Biblical Doctrine of Infant Baptism, you will have a treat of sound Covenant Theology. But I must also say that, despite all the benefits that Covenant Theology presents us with, it is only one part of the story. I believe a fuller explanation of the actual points in debate, built upon the framework of the covenant, is the most persuasive argument for Paedobaptism. In this book, I attempt to do just that.

Covenant Theology is, however, a relatively new construct. While I believe its principles are found throughout the Bible, it was never really systematized until after the Reformation. Its power is clearly seen by the fact that so many Reformed Baptists in our day wish to embrace Covenant Theology themselves. Almost every book published on Credobaptism tries to make Covenant Theology their own. There are a host of new books on this supposed Credobaptist "Covenantal Theology." It's funny; they all realize the benefits of Covenant Theology, and they want it; but they have to manipulate it to fit their Baptist thinking. I have two of these books on my desk (I can't buy them all; there are too many), and neither one is Covenantal in their thinking. Sure, they aren't dispensational either; but call it something else, because it's not Covenant Theology. You can't remove a core element of Biblical Covenants, namely they always included the persons covenanting *and their descendants*, and then expect anyone to take your "Covenant Theology" seriously. Both of these authors state as a reason for writing their books, that they wish to stop the loss of so many of their Baptist seminarians to the Paedobaptist persuasion. Neither one, of course, even postulates that it might be because the Paedobaptists have the better argument. I submit this as a better argument, and a reason why all of their seminarians should come over to the Paedobaptist side.

Lastly, it's a popular Credobaptist argument to claim that the practice of Paedobaptism makes for an impure church. And if we take a look at what the Reformers were reforming from, we can see why they would think that way. There were thousands of baptized pagans walking around, all claiming membership in the "Church," but none of them living a life worthy of the title "Christian." In response to this atrocity, the Anabaptists sought to "purify" the Church by only baptizing those who could give good evidence of their conversion. I cannot doubt their good intentions. Some of those men are my heroes. However, while the contention for a pure church had some merit at that time, today it's completely devoid of such merit. When you look out into the so-called evangelical Church today, I am sure you'll agree that we see a bunch of worldly pagans all calling themselves "Christians." Yet out of the millions that claim the name, only a handful could prove that claim with a corresponding lifestyle. And out of all of those millions of baptized pagans, the vast majority, in America anyway, were baptized after confession. That is not to mention all of the doctrinal errors that are associated with this as well. Notice that all of the "Christian" cults, such as Mormons and Jehovah's Witnesses, only baptize professing adults and refuse to baptize infants. The prosperity Gospel, the Charismatic movement, and the mega-church movement are all Credobaptists. Now, does that mean that the Credobaptist position on baptism is wrong? Of course not. But neither did it mean that Paedobaptism was wrong in the Reformation. The tables have turned. The insistence of a pure church membership hasn't helped the Baptists in America, and now it's time to re-examine their position.

I do not claim to be the first who has taught the things included in this book; I am only standing on the shoulders of Christian giants who have come before me. I have very little new material to add to what has been said in the past; I am only going to take what I have learned and present it in my own style for the sake of being personal. But I must also say that the arguments contained in this book are confronting long held and very personal beliefs that are just not true, and because of this, you may get vehement reactions to it. When you have people who are committed to a certain position have their arguments for that position proven wrong, they tend not to give up on their position, they give up on *arguing*. So use this information wisely and cautiously to avoid actually stepping on too many toes and to be sensitive to your brothers feelings. Remember, it's about the truth, it's not about proving yourself to be the holder of that truth.

~ Andrew W. Camp

"The first one to plead his cause seems right, until his neighbor comes and examines him."
(Proverbs 18:17)

Chapter 1

PRELIMINARY ISSUES

Let's start with the basics. Proverbs 18:17 illustrates what I believe to be the most significant principle that a Paedobaptist apologist will need to get across to his Credobaptist brother. "The first one to plead his cause seems right, until his neighbor comes and examines him." Most of us will naturally hear someone argue a particular position from Scripture, and will receive it instantly without first hearing the other positions on that topic. We all know that we are supposed to believe what Scripture teaches us; so as long as the argument we hear is reasonably cogent, we will accept it. It's natural; we all do it. Usually, it's our parents who give us our first instruction from the Scriptures, and we fully trust them (rightly so) because they seem to know everything. However, when we grow up, we realize that our parents were fallible and could very well have been wrong. The first arguments that we hear *always* sound right! It's only when someone else steps in and points out the faults in the argument, that we start to think, "Maybe I was a bit rash…" We would all be much wiser if we would only pay attention to this simple Proverb.

Our Credobaptist brethren tell us that there is no command in Scripture to baptize our infants. They tell us that there is no example of it in the Bible.[1] They tell us that immersion is the only mode of baptism possible. I flat-out deny all of these assertions, and boldly state that the Bible certainly *does* command us to have our children

---

[1] Surprisingly, some of my Paedobaptist brethren agree with these Credobaptists. Our Credobaptist brethren are fond of quoting such persons.

baptized. It certainly *does* give us examples, and the *only mode* of baptism in the entire Bible is *effusion*. We will be proving these assertions throughout this book, along with so much more. But first, we need to make sure we are all on the same sheet of music. I don't pretend to think that everyone reading this book will have the exact same nuanced theological positions that I have. But with that being said, there are a few core theological positions that will be very helpful background in any discussion with our Credobaptist brethren. In this chapter, we are going to examine and support those positions. If you already hold to them, then you can either keep reading so that you can get a refresher, or you can skip this part and get to the meat of the argument in Chapter 2.

I like to ask Baptists, "When was the last time you read a book on why we *should* baptize our children?" From my own experience as a Baptist, I know I had never done so. I simply assumed that the arguments that I had been taught for the "confessing adults only" position were true because they sounded good to me. After all, the arguments seemed reasonable, and I couldn't think of any opposing arguments. And if I couldn't think of any opposing arguments, there must not be any, right? The Baptists were the "first ones to plead their cause" to me, and they seemed right. I considered the Baptist position to be so airtight that I didn't even want to waste my time reading what those "infant baptizers" thought. A few years later, by the grace of God, a "neighbor" who just happened to be an "infant baptizer" came along and examined those beliefs.

I remember, quite clearly, my first encounter with a real live *knowledgeable* Paedobaptist.[1] I say "knowledgeable," because I had met plenty of Paedobaptists who couldn't give me a reason to wake up in the morning, let alone a reason to baptize my infants. This knowledgeable Paedobaptist was the pastor of a Presbyterian church (PCA) in Wichita, Kansas, who had been a Baptist minister himself some years previous.[2] He started to talk to me about these issues, and I was at once impressed with his knowledge. He spoke, and I

---

[1] *Paedobaptist* refers to those who practice baptizing infants (*paedo* = child).
[2] He was kind enough to write the foreword to this book.

listened. What he said was interesting, but I was no pushover and I was ready for him. He quit speaking and then…it was *my* turn. I unleashed my fury and gave him everything I had! I mean, I pulled out all of my guns, unloaded both barrels on him, and left him for dead! As the smoke cleared, I saw that he was still alive…but no man could have survived the onslaught that I had just unleashed…he had a look on his face that said, "Is that the best you can do?" Then, without missing a beat, he proceeded to take every argument that I had, and grind it into *dust*. I felt like a schoolboy as he told me things that I had never heard of nor considered. I walked away from our conversation-battle, worn-out and scarred; he had won the battle…*but I would win the war!* I poured myself into the study of both positions, Credobaptist and Paedobaptist. In the end, my conclusion was that I could not debate with the Paedobaptist arguments because they were *consistently Biblical;* and my Credobaptist position was not even logically consistent, let alone Biblical. I had fooled myself into thinking that if *I* couldn't think of a good reason for the Credobaptist arguments to be wrong, then there must not be *anybody* that can think of a good reason that the Credobaptist arguments are wrong. Praise God that I had a "neighbor" who was willing to "examine" my beliefs!

I, for one, have learned my lesson. I now counsel every Christian I know, to first examine every position thoroughly before firmly taking sides on any theological topic.[1] Think about it; how many times have you said, or heard someone say, about a particular Scripture, "How can they not understand this?" or "This passage is so clear! How can they not see?" Consider that maybe it's *you* that cannot see. Maybe it's *your* understanding of that passage that is flawed. Do you think that those people who supposedly "don't understand" have never read those passages of Scripture? So maybe you should be asking *them* how *they* understand those passages. You may be surprised at the answers you get.

---

[1] To clarify: I do believe that it is proper to accept the Word of God without first examining all positions, but here I am speaking about Christian arguments over theological positions.

"For the Bible tells me so"

Sing it with me…"Jesus loves me this I know…" That's right, you finished it in your mind, didn't you? "For the Bible tells me so." The Bible is a glorious book! I confess along with my Reformed brethren everywhere…

> …that this Holy Scripture fully contains the will of God and that all that man must believe in order to be saved is sufficiently taught therein. The whole manner of worship which God requires of us is written in it at length. It is therefore unlawful for anyone, even for an apostle, to teach otherwise than we are now taught in Holy Scripture: yes, even if it be an angel from heaven, as the apostle Paul says. Since it is forbidden to add to or take away anything from the Word of God, it is evident that the doctrine thereof is most perfect and complete in all respects.

I don't think you will run into many Credobaptists who would disagree with the above statement from the Belgic Confession of Faith.[1] We all rightly hold to the Holy Scriptures as our highest authority. What it teaches, we believe. What it commands, we do. Indeed, it is (or should be) treated by all Christians as what it itself claims to be: the very *Word of God*. But given the sheer number of different opinions in the Church, we need to propose a pertinent question. What counts as Holy Scripture? Just reach up and pull a Bible off the shelf, and there you have it, right? Most would answer that way and be right…I think. It depends on their answers to a few additional questions, to see if they really hold that Book to be the Word of God. And until you get answers to those questions, there is no point in continuing. We all have to have the same starting point, in order to reason together.

The first question is this: Is the Bible inspired in its entirety? Is it Holy Scripture from front cover to back? Is even the *Old*

---

[1] By the way, the writers of that confession were Paedobaptists.

Testament profitable for doctrine? (2 Tim. 3:16) I hope they will agree with you in saying, "Yes, it is inspired in its entirety." Yet there are many who hold to a pseudo-inspiration of the Old Testament or other passages of Scripture. For instance, some will say that the Old Testament is no longer applicable to "New Testament" Christians. The heretic Marcion from the second century AD was the first that we know of, who took the view that the Old Testament was not applicable to Christians. He has been followed by many today, such as those in the Church of Christ denomination. Of course, there are differences between the Old Testament and the New, but the Old is still absolutely the inspired Word of God. To Marcion, and to many today, the Old Testament represented another time, and is wholly inapplicable to Christians today.

Have you ever wondered what the first-century Christians had as their Bible? They obviously did not have the Bible that we have, since it was still being written. The Christians that heard the Apostle Peter speak on the day of Pentecost, only had what we refer to today as the *Old* Testament. That was it. They had no Gospel according to Matthew; no Epistle to the Romans; they only had the books of the Old Testament. *But*, they also had the Apostles there to help explain those Scriptures to them. Do you know what Bible the second-century Christians had? They had the Old Testament with the Apostles' *writings* to help explain it to them. You see, the Apostles thought that the Old Testament *was* the Word of God and had all the authority of God. Notice what the Apostle Paul said in 2 Timothy 3:16:

> All Scripture is given by inspiration of God, and is profitable for doctrine, for reproof, for correction, for instruction in righteousness, that the man of God may be complete, thoroughly equipped for every good work.

What "Scripture" was the Apostle Paul speaking about? Do you think he had your King James Bible in mind? Of course not; he was referring to the Old Testament. The New Testament was not even written yet. Read through the New Testament epistles; and you will see the Apostles explaining the Old Testament, addressing contemporary issues with the Old Testament, and encouraging Christians from the Old Testament. We Christians have hope "through the patience and comfort of the Scriptures," meaning the Old Testament (Rom. 15:4). Over and over again, the Apostles lifted up the Old Testament as the inspired Word of God, perfectly applicable to all areas of our Christian lives. Every Christian doctrine that an Apostle teaches in the New Testament, is supported by the Old Testament. When the Apostle Paul wanted to teach justification by faith alone, to what authority did he appeal? When Peter wanted to instruct women in their proper role, to what did he appeal? The book of Hebrews is one big sermon from Old Testament texts. I could go on and on. The Apostles supported their teachings with the Word of God, being the Old Testament. I am sure that at some point in all of our Christian lives, we have been encouraged to "be a Berean" and "search the Scriptures" to see if something is so.[1] It's good advice; but remember, the Bereans were searching the Old Testament! So, if Credobaptists do not view the Old Testament in the same way that the Apostles did, you might have problems trying to reason with that person as you appeal from Scripture.

Here is the second question we must ask: Are some parts of Scripture more authoritative than others? For instance, I had one Christian brother tell me once that he believes that the words of Christ, as recorded in the Gospels, carry more authority than what the Apostles say in the New Testament epistles. This, of course, is impossible. We only know what Christ said, because the Apostles *told* us what He said. This belief also betrays an awful understanding of inspiration. The whole of Scripture is the Word of God, not just when it says, "Thus saith the Lord." When an Apostle speaks in Scripture, it's just as authoritative as when Jesus speaks in Scripture. Those who believe differently usually do so because they believe that the teachings of the Bible are sometimes contradictory. "Paul said this, *but* Jesus said that." Once I had a conversation with someone, in which I quoted a passage from one of Paul's epistles. The reply I

---

[1] Acts 17:11.

received was, "Yes, but that's Paul. What did *Jesus* say?" As if Paul ever disagreed with what Christ taught! Of course, that is not the case. All Scripture is the very Word of God; none of it is contradictory, and all of it is authoritative. The Apostles were commissioned by Christ Himself, and so they carry His authority.

To be sure, there are things in the Old Testament that are no longer our ruling precepts. God's people are no longer bound to a specific geographic location; God has thrown open the doors of salvation so that people from all nations can come in. And in so doing, He had to remove the wall of division that was between them. So while there are many non-continuities between the Old Testament and the New (such as Sabbaths, sacrifices, and food restrictions), there are also many continuities which are eternal. I would contend that one of those continuities is Covenant succession. So, where do we find specific instructions which tell us that our children are no longer part of the people of God, as they were in the Old Testament? On the contrary, the same theme is continued into the New Testament: "to you and to your seed." We will see much more about this later.

I once had some dear Baptist friends try to convince me that infant baptism was wrong, by reading me a story about how an Anabaptist martyr had a dream, and his dream came true; thus "proving" that the Anabaptist position is the correct one. I find it ironic that some people claim to get their theology straight from the Bible, and then they present proof of their theological assertions from antiquated stories. This particular story was even written in poetry. If I were to tell you that I had a dream, in which I was going to have a burning feeling in my bosom that would verify my beliefs; and then, when I woke up, I actually had that burning in my bosom; would you then believe my views? Or would you simply say, "Andrew, you had heartburn and nothing else." You see, no matter how much we appeal to esoteric feelings or stories of supposedly miraculous events, we must always judge a doctrine by the Word of God, and the Word of God *only*.

"DO YOU EVEN HAVE A VERSE?"

I once told a Baptist minister, who had come to my home for a visit, that I had changed my views from Credobaptism[1] to Paedobaptism; and with a look of abject horror on his face, he exclaimed, "Do you even have a verse?!"

Maybe some of my readers have had similar experiences. And some of the Credobaptists whom you engage are going to recognize that form of interrogation. "Do they even have a verse?" Well, the answer to that question from the Paedobaptist side is a resounding "Yes!" We have lots of verses. But let me first point out that when that Baptist minister asked that question, he betrayed a deep-rooted unbiblical belief that the Bible is a book of proof-texts. The proof-text mentality has misled thousands of people into believing that if the Bible doesn't *say* it, then it's not true. If you believe that to be the case, you have been misled. A Christian should never say, "If the Bible doesn't *say* it, I won't believe it!" That's false. A Christian says, "If the Bible doesn't *teach* it, I won't believe it." *That* is correct.

I hope you understand the difference. The Bible *teaches* things that it does not necessarily explicitly *say*. The Bible is not to be treated as a systematic theology. It is not all didactic; if it were, we would have no debates. We would just look up the chapter on the sacraments, find the heading "Proper Recipients of Baptism," and read to see if infants are to be baptized. We can't do that. We need to find out what the Bible *teaches* on the subject, and you don't do that with a proof-text mentality. You must come to the same understanding of the Scriptures that the writers themselves had. To do that, you must let the Bible speak for itself and define its own terms. When the Biblical authors used a particular term, we are not to believe that we can use our own definition for that term; rather, we must let the Bible define that term if at all possible. "The Bible is

---

[1] A Credobaptist is one who believes that a person must make a statement of faith (*credo* = creed or belief) before that person is baptized. Thus, they rule out infants from the Sacrament.

its own best interpreter." We have all heard that creed before; but we don't often live by it, as we will see in a later section.

Let me give you an example to make this point very clear. Everybody knows who the Jehovah's Witnesses are: those nice people who come to your door and show you cartoon pictures of a bunch of happy people in a "paradise on earth." Yeah, that's them. No matter how you appeal to them from Scripture to prove to them that the Scriptures do indeed teach Christ's deity, they will refuse to believe it because the Bible doesn't *say it*. Another topic on which you will hear them spew out their ignorance, is the Trinity. You will hear the JW's say consistently, "The word *Trinity* isn't even in the Bible." They hope to impress upon us their misguided idea that the Bible must not *teach* that God is a Trinity, because the Bible doesn't *say* the word *Trinity*. This reasoning is absurd. The Bible also does not include the words *Christianity, theology, depravity, omnipresent, transcendence, theophany, Christophany, philanthropy, duothelitism, dichotomy, antinomianism, monarchy,* etc. All of these words, and others, have theological meaning that is derived from the teaching of the Scriptures; and although none of them are found *in* Scripture, they are all derived *from* Scripture.

Thus, to get to my point, we are to strive to understand what the Bible *teaches*. You must not reject the Biblical doctrine of baptism simply because the Bible does not *say*, "Thou shalt baptize your infants." You must find out what the Bible teaches on baptism as a whole, and believe that. Have you ever read the Scripture that says, "Jesus is God"? I didn't think so. Thus, I hope to show you that the Bible does indeed *teach* that we are to baptize our infants, just as clearly as it teaches that Jesus is God.

If you are in a faithful church, you should have been taught that the Bible is authoritative in what it teaches—both explicitly and implicitly. The implicitly taught doctrines, such as the Triune nature of God, are just as important and relevant as the explicitly taught doctrines, such as the oneness of God. If you miss the implicit, you open yourself up to error on all sides.

FEDERAL HEADSHIP

In order to properly understand the nature of children throughout the Bible, we need to make very clear the theological theme called Federal Headship. Although you won't find the phrase "Federal Headship" in Scripture, I am sure that you will agree that it is clearly taught throughout the Bible.

Have you ever wondered why the Bible doesn't say that sin came from Eve? After all, she sinned first, right? Well, there really is no good answer for that, except for the doctrine of Federal Headship. It was Adam who was the representative of the human race, not Eve. Adam was the head of his wife, and not vice versa as Satan would have it to be. God has set up this authority structure for many reasons, not the least of which is that God Himself has this structure in His own Triune nature. Father, Son and Holy Spirit are all equally God; and yet the Son submits to the Father, and the Spirit submits to the Father and the Son, for the sake of function. This is what we are taught in Philippians 2.

Adam was the representative for the whole human race; and so when he sinned, we all sinned *in* him. I use that term "in" for a specific reason that you will soon see. First, however, let me tell you about a man named David who slew a giant. Of course, you all know the story of David and Goliath, and how David killed this giant of a man with only a stone. We can see from the outset that Federal Headship was suggested by Goliath. He proclaimed these words to all Israel:

> Choose a man for yourselves, and let him come down to me. If he is able to fight with me and kill me, then we will be your servants. But if I prevail against him and kill him, then you shall be our servants and serve us (1 Sam. 17:8, 9).

This is the perfect example of Federal Headship; one representing the many, or the many being *in* one. I remember when I was a child, learning about the various wars that our country had been in; and I would ask my father, "Why don't we just have our president and their president fight, and then the winner will win the war?" Simple solution, isn't it? Unknowingly, I was suggesting Federal Headship, just as Goliath had suggested it.

Let's make a small change to the story of David and Goliath, in order to help flesh out and illustrate this doctrine of Federal Headship. Let's imagine the impossible. Let's imagine that David lost the fight, and all of Israel became the slaves of the Philistines, per Goliath's challenge. Now what would they do? Let's look at this in a purely illustrative sense, and not in an actual sense; because we all know that just as the Philistines ran away after Goliath had been defeated, so would Israel have fled if David had been defeated. So in keeping with our illustration, we will imagine that David lost, and all of Israel truly became slaves. How would the Israelites ever get out of slavery? Could another man in Israel stand up and say, "Hey, I don't like the way that David fought; he was just a kid! Let me fight Goliath and see who wins!" No, he couldn't. Why? Because he is already a slave of the Philistines. What right does a slave have of challenging a king? The king of Israel had already chosen a representative for their nation, and they must stick by it. Legally speaking, all of the Israelites were "in" David, and all of the Philistines were "in" Goliath. So when David (hypothetically) lost, all of the Israelites lost (in him) and were made slaves of the Philistines. A slave has no legal right to try again for his freedom. Goliath would have laughed at any such attempt and said, "Why should I give you another chance? You are already my slaves." Even all of the infants born to the Israelites after this, were legally Israelites, and thus slaves. So how could they ever be free again? It would take someone from outside of Israel, who was not represented by David, to come and try to free the Israelites. Someone to come and say to Goliath, "I am not your slave, and so I challenge you to a fight for the Israelites' freedom." We have seen that Someone in the person of Jesus Christ.

That illustration answers for us some of the deepest questions that are asked by believers all the time, such as, "Why didn't Eve pass on sin?" "Why did Adam sin and I suffer for it?" "Why doesn't God give me a chance to try to live perfectly?" "Why can't I pay for my own sins?" "Is it fair that we all suffer because one man sinned?" "Why did Jesus have to be born of a virgin?" You see, Adam was your representative before God. Eve was not. Adam's challenge was to walk perfectly before his God. He failed and threw all of those whom he represented into a state of sin; slaves to sin, if you will. When you were born, you were legally "in" Adam, and thus a slave to sin. You could not even try to earn your freedom, because you are already a slave. It took Jesus Christ to come, "born of a virgin"—not in Adam's line, and so not legally a slave to sin. Jesus took the same challenge Adam did, and succeeded in living perfectly before God, thereby making a way to free the slaves. If we had not all fallen "in" Adam, then we would not all be able to live "in" Christ. The Scripture says:

> For if by the one man's offense many died, much more the grace of God and the gift by the grace of the one Man, Jesus Christ, abounded to many (Rom. 5:15).

And,

> In Adam all die, even so in Christ all shall be made alive (1 Cor. 15:22).

Examples of the doctrine of Federal Headship abound in the Scriptures. God has placed the man in the family unit as the federal head of his household. That means that God placed the responsibility of everything that a man's household did or does, squarely on the shoulders of the father. If the father was a Jew, the whole family was Jewish. It seems strange to our western Baptistic ways; but we must remember to interpret Scripture the way Scripture presents itself, not in our own modern ways. Adam was the father of the whole human race. He sinned; and in him, we all sinned.

Joshua was the father and federal head of his household. If he decided to follow Jehovah, the whole household was to follow Jehovah.

> And if it seems evil to you to serve the Lord, choose for yourselves this day whom you will serve, whether the gods which your fathers

served that were on the other side of the River, or the gods of the Amorites, in whose land you dwell. **But as for me and my house, we will serve the Lord** (Josh. 24:15).

Joshua made the decision for his household; he didn't take a vote. His house would follow the Lord, simply because *he* was going to follow the Lord.

Please consider with me what happened on the night of the first Passover, when the children of Israel were preparing to leave Egypt. The Lord told each head of household to take a lamb, slay it, and sprinkle the blood on the two doorposts and on the lintel of the house. By doing this, the head of household would save his family from the death of the firstborn. Then that head of household was to lead his household from Egypt to the Promised Land. Where is the faith of the infants in all this? They experienced the salvation, but what was their role? Nothing; they were under the headship of their father, and their role was simply to keep the faith once they left Egypt. I suggest that this is the same thing in our Christian homes; the father has put his house under the protection of the blood of Christ, and then he has led his family out of the world where they were in bondage. The children's role is simply to keep the faith of their father, or else to fall away.

Chapter 2

DISMANTLING THE CREDOBAPTIST ARGUMENT

Now we enter into the shock-and-awe portion of the debate. A Credobaptist needs to see, *from Scripture,* why their position is demonstrably false. This chapter is meant to give you the arsenal to do such. There is a host of minutia that can and will be dealt with in later chapters;[1] but right now you need to use your big artillery, and wake the Credobaptist up to the realization that the foundation their theory is built upon is a foundation of sand. Now of course, we must always remember to be gracious to our Credobaptist brethren; but at this phase of the debate, it's essential to shake their presuppositions so badly that the worldview lenses through which they view this topic start to fall from their eyes. They need to come to a place where they are questioning their own presuppositions. This rarely happens in the debate, because most encounters between Credo and Paedo focus on the minutia of the argument. These issues are only to be discussed after you have their attention, and have shown them that they can't trust what they have been taught in their tradition.

---

[1] "Everything cannot be disproved at once. And when Baptist writers flee from their present falling house, to some other refuge, and cry, "But you have not shaken down this," we can only answer, Get fixed in your new quarters and wait your turn." James W. Dale, Judaic Baptism pg 119.

BELIEVE AND BE BAPTIZED

So let's start our nuclear destruction of the Credobaptist position with the first salvo. Let's start with their logical *Magnus opus*, and dismantle it for all to see. The Credobaptist will usually argue very simply in this fashion...

Premise 1: You must believe to be baptized.
Premise 2: Infants can't believe.
Conclusion: Therefore, infants cannot be baptized.

You need to get the Credobaptist to agree with that syllogism; which, of course, should be no problem, since it comes right from their own sources.[1] But you may get tangled up with a Credobaptist who will try to make things hard on you and say, "No, it's not that; it's such-and-such..." Let them give you the syllogism; that's fine. They will all be the same syllogism. For example, if they say that you must first show signs of regeneration prior to baptism, then use the following syllogism:

Premise 1: You must show signs of regeneration to be baptized.
Premise 2: Infants can't show signs of regeneration.
Conclusion: Therefore, infants cannot be baptized.

You see? It doesn't matter how they wish to frame it. Their syllogism is always the same. It's quite easy to understand, and quite

---

[1] One of those sources would be Wayne Grudem: "The pattern revealed at several places in the New Testament is that only those who give a believable profession of faith should be baptized." Wayne Grudem, Systematic Theology pg 969
So...
Premise 1: You must give a believable profession of faith in order to be baptized.
Premise 2: Infants can't give a believable profession of faith.
Conclusion: Therefore, infants should not be baptized.

persuasive when used by a knowledgeable Credobaptist against the common Paedobaptist. We can all see the relevance and power of the argument. The problem is not that it is not persuasive; if it weren't, there wouldn't be a Baptist church on every corner. The problem is that it's *false*. So when you are confronted with this argument, you need to show the Credobaptist that the actual logical syllogism is *Biblically* false. That is, it may look good when it's written out or stated in a syllogism; but when it's put up against the Bible, we see that the syllogism is woefully incorrect.

This is how you dismantle their argument. Have them open their Bible to Numbers, chapter 6, and repeat their syllogism to them.

> The Bible says to believe and be baptized;
> infants can't believe;
> therefore, we don't baptize them.

Now explain to them that Paedobaptists are not particularly moved by this line of argumentation, because they are used to thinking in bigger categories. You see, the pattern is irrelevant when we turn our discussion to children. They are in a different category, and don't always fit into the adult patterns.

Now read verses 1-8, and give them an example to prove the assertion and demonstrate the falsity of the Credo logic. Numbers 6:1-8 records for us the law of the Nazirite.

> Then the LORD spoke to Moses, saying, "Speak to the children of Israel, and say to them: **'When either a man or woman consecrates an offering to take the vow of a Nazirite,** to separate himself to the LORD, **he shall separate himself from wine and similar drink**; he shall drink neither vinegar made from wine nor vinegar made from similar drink; neither shall he drink any grape juice, nor eat fresh grapes or raisins. All the days of his separation he shall eat nothing that is produced by the grapevine, from seed to skin. All the days of the vow of his separation no razor shall come upon his head; until the days are fulfilled for which he separated himself to the LORD, he shall be holy. Then he shall let the locks of the hair of his head grow. All the days that he separates

himself to the LORD he shall not go near a dead body. He shall not make himself unclean even for his father or his mother, for his brother or his sister, when they die, because his separation to God is on his head. All the days of his separation he shall be holy to the LORD.'"

As you can see, it clearly states that Nazirites are to "vow," "separate themselves," "not make himself unclean," "eat nothing that is produced by the grapevine," "let the locks of the hair of his head grow," etc. It stresses the fact that this vow is to be made by the person vowing, and no one can vow for that person, since it states four times, "separate *himself*." I submit to you that an infant cannot do any of those things. This is clearly an example of a volitional state of being if there ever was one. You must "separate yourself" and "vow," in order to be a Nazirite. Therefore, an infant cannot be a Nazirite if we follow the very logic that Credobaptists propose.

Premise 1: You must vow (etc.) to be a Nazirite.

Premise 2: Infants can't vow (etc.)

Conclusion: Therefore, Infants cannot be Nazirites.

This is the only place where God lays down the Nazirite law, and it clearly spells out that being a Nazirite is *volitional,* a matter of the *will.* But wait…the next place we see the word Nazirite in the Bible, it is referring to Samson. And what do we find there?

And the Angel of the LORD appeared to the woman and said to her, "Indeed now, you are barren and have borne no children, but you shall conceive and bear a son. Now therefore, please **be careful not to drink wine or similar drink, and not to eat anything unclean.** For behold, you shall conceive and bear a son. And no razor shall come upon his head, **for the child shall be a Nazirite to God from the womb;** and he shall begin to deliver Israel out of the hand of the Philistines." So the woman came and told her husband, saying, "A Man of God came to me, and His countenance was like the countenance of the Angel of God, very awesome; but I did not ask

Him where He was from, and He did not tell me His name. And He said to me, 'Behold, you shall conceive and bear a son. **Now drink no wine or similar drink, nor eat anything unclean, for the child shall be a Nazirite to God from the womb to the day of his death**'" (Jud. 13:3-7).

Well now, I guess the Baptist logic doesn't work, now does it? God specifically demanded volition to become a Nazirite. He demanded a "vow," and the ability to "separate" and "keep clean"; and none of that can be done by an infant, let alone a pre-born infant. So how can this be? How can God contradict Himself? How can Samson be a Nazirite from the womb, when he can't "vow," "separate himself," or "keep clean"? Well, the answer is the same answer to the Credo's pattern of "believe in order to be baptized." *The parents fulfill those things for the child.* Notice that the angel told the mother to "be careful not to drink wine or similar drink," and that "no razor shall come upon his head." The mother fulfills the obligation for the baby. This is assumed throughout Scripture. I wonder if, during the hundreds of years between Moses and Samson, there were ever Credo-Nazirites. "Of course you can't make that baby a Nazirite; he can't even vow!" So if the logic that is espoused by Credobaptists is true, we would expect that Samson could not have been a Nazirite until he himself was old enough to make a vow.

I'm a Paedo-Nazirite. The parent of the child can take the vow for the child, and keep themselves clean of wine and keep a razor from the child's head, until such a time as the child takes on the responsibility for himself. In the case of baptism, the parent fulfills the obligations for his child (repent, believe, and confess) and makes him a disciple. Then he baptizes him, per the command of Christ. Note that as long as *his mother* kept the vow, *the child* was a Nazirite.

But lo, we are not finished with this line of reasoning! Lest it be argued that God made this happen and not Samson's parents, notice that Hannah also dedicated her pre-conceived babe to the life of a Nazirite: "No razor shall come upon his head" (1 Sam. 1:11). *She* made the decision *for her son,* and God blessed her. According to the text she made the required vow for her son, and she kept the razor from his head. Then there is also the case of John the Baptizer, whom most believe was a Nazirite from the womb. So please tell me, why can't I dedicate my child to a life of service to God, and have him baptized as a disciple?

Therefore, either it was wrong for Samson, Samuel, and John the Baptizer to have been Nazirites from the womb; or else the Baptist syllogism is flat-out *false*. We must beg our Credobaptist brethren's forgiveness for our preference of the Scriptures over their argument.

Notice that this is exactly what the Christian church has maintained that Christian parents do for their children *in baptism*. The Anglican Catechism of 1549 stated it quite clearly, by addressing a young person coming to their confirmation:

Q. What is your name?

A. N. or M.

Q. Who gave you this Name?

A. My Godfathers and Godmothers **in my Baptism;** wherein I was made a member of Christ, the child of God, and an inheritor of the Kingdom of heaven.

Q. What did your Godfathers and Godmothers then for you?

A. **They did promise and vow three things in my name.** First, that I should renounce the devil and all his works and pomps, the vanities of the wicked world, and all the sinful lusts of the flesh. Secondly, that I should believe all the Articles of the Christian Faith. And thirdly, that I should keep God's holy will and commandments, and walk in the same all the days of my life.

Q. Dost thou not think that thou art bound to believe, and to do, **as they have promised for thee?**

A. Yes verily; and by God's help so I will. And I heartily thank our heavenly Father, that he has called me to this state of salvation, through Jesus Christ our Savior. And I pray God to give me his grace, that I may continue in the same unto my life's end.

We see in this catechetical exchange that, just like the Nazirite, the parents[1] made the necessary vows for the child; and the child was thus made a member of Christ, and a child of God. The child's role was to continue in and complete the path he was already put into. The vows that the parents made for the child are the same vows an adult convert would have made to receive baptism; and the vows that the mother of Samson had to fulfill for Samson were the same vows recorded in Numbers 6 for an adult Nazirite.

As we go through Scripture, we can see similar circumstances in which Christian parents fulfilled obligations for their children. We see this very noticeably in circumcision. Paul boasts about his circumcision in Philippians 3:5; but it was his parents that did that for him. We'll explore that a bit more in the next section; but for now, let's look at what Paul says in Galatians.

And I testify again to every man who becomes circumcised that he is a debtor to keep the whole law (Gal. 5:3).

Can an infant be a debtor? Can an infant keep the law? Of course not; his parents kept it for him. Millions of grown adults were debtors to their faithful parents, who had kept the covenant for their children.

In addition, if the Credobaptist logic were accurate, all of their children would starve because...

If anyone will not work, neither shall he eat (2 Thess. 3:10).

A *consistent* Baptist would interpret this passage in this way:

Premise 1: "If anyone will not work, neither shall he eat."
Premise 2: "Infants cannot work."
Conclusion: "And so they should not eat."

---

[1] *Godparents* would have been the child's parents, or any relative that would stand in for the parents when they were deceased.

The syllogism is the same. "No workie—no eatie." Simple. If Baptists were consistent, they would have no children at all because they would all starve. Thank God that they are not *that* consistent.

All right, you know how you want to answer that, don't you? You want to say, "But that verse is obviously speaking about adults." Well, of course it is. Anybody with common sense can see that. But this verse is also speaking about adults:

> He who believes and is baptized will be saved; but he who does not believe will be condemned (Mark 16:16).

The early Church was a mission church. *Everyone* was an adult convert; so of course the Bible is going to speak to the *adults*.[1] Point out to the Credobaptist that there are no examples in Scripture of someone who was raised in a Christian home and then baptized as an adult.

Paedobaptists, on the other hand, remain absolutely consistent in their interpretation of these verses. It is the fathers that are responsible for the family, and so they are the ones that must work in order to eat. If the father did not work, his whole family did not eat. If the father worked hard, his whole family benefited from his work...they ate. In the same sense, it is the father that is responsible for his family in the spiritual realm as well. If the father had faith, the whole family benefited from his faith—they ate spiritually. The father fulfilled the obligations of work for his children. If he didn't, they didn't eat.

Of course, you know that if you were talking to a Credobaptist about 2 Thessalonians 3:10, and you told him, "This text is only speaking about adults, and so we do not need to apply it to infants," he wouldn't bat an eye. He would accept that as a perfectly sound judgment on a text that could potentially confuse someone if it were

---

[1] What happens in a mission church when the converts have children? Household baptisms, of course.

wrongly interpreted. But then say, "Mark 16:16 is speaking to adults only, and so we should not apply it to infants," and you will have a huge problem on your hands. Why? Because Baptists interpret one verse differently than the other, solely on the basis of a presupposition. But Paedobaptists acknowledge that these verses are spoken *to the adults only,* and so we are not left trying to reconcile any contradictions.

Furthermore, if the Credobaptist logic were correct, then no elders in the Church would be allowed to have babies. Oh, they could have children, to be sure; but no infants. Notice that in the only two places where the requirements for elders are presented, a bishop (or elder) must be...

> ...one who rules his own house well, **having his children in submission with all reverence** (1Tim. 3:4).

> ...the husband of one wife, **having faithful children** not accused of dissipation or insubordination (Tit. 1:6).

I submit to you the incontrovertible truth, that an infant is not capable of *submission, reverence,* or *faithfulness.* Therefore, based upon Credobaptist logic, elders are not allowed to have babies. They can have children that meet those requirements, but not infants who cannot meet those requirements. So his wife had better be beyond child-bearing age; because if she gets pregnant, her husband is out of a job. See? Ridiculous, isn't it? But press the Credobaptist to demonstrate to you how that doesn't fit his logical syllogism.

> *Premise 1:* In order to be an elder, you must have children that are submissive, reverent and faithful.
> *Premise 2:* Infants cannot submit, be reverent, or be faithful.
> *Conclusion:* Therefore, elders cannot have infants.

Why is it that we don't ever hear Credobaptists refusing their pastors the right to have infant children? Well, it's simple, isn't it? By nature, we *know* that if the parent is faithful, the children are to be *reckoned* faithful as well, until such a time as they prove otherwise. We do this every day without even thinking about it. It's only when it comes in stark contradiction to a beloved theory, that the Credobaptist rejects common-sense language and adopts this unbiblical logical syllogism. Perhaps some other real-world examples would help demonstrate this.

Premise 1: For a non-American to enter the United States, that person must promise to obey American laws.
Premise 2: Infants cannot promise to obey American laws.
Conclusion: Therefore, no infants can ever enter the United States.

Premise 1: I invite you to "walk on over to my house for dinner."
Premise 2: Infants cannot walk.
Conclusion: Therefore, you must leave your infants at home.

Premise 1: At a hotel, all guests must adhere to safety rules.
Premise 2: Infants cannot adhere to safety rules.
Conclusion: Therefore, infants cannot be guests in a hotel.

Premise 1: You must speak Romanian to be a Romanian citizen.
Premise 2: Infants cannot speak Romanian.
Conclusion: Therefore, infants cannot be Romanian citizens.

Premise 1: Jesus said, "Let the little children come to Me" for a blessing.
Premise 2: Infants cannot *come*.
Conclusion: Therefore, Jesus never blessed an infant.[1]

---

[1] Of course, when Jesus said this, the parents "brought" infants to Him (Luke 18:15). This shows that parents can fulfil the requirement for the child. See section "Can they come to Jesus?"

Premise 1: You must purchase a ticket to ride a bus.
Premise 2: Infants cannot purchase anything.
Conclusion: Therefore, infants cannot ride a bus.

Examples can be multiplied; and I'm sure that even your Credobaptist brethren can think of examples on their own. But please drive this point home to your Credobaptist brother. In everyday life situations, *a Credobaptist consistently thinks like a Paedobaptist.* But when their theory hangs in the balance, they will reject the common-sense inclusion of infants (which they use in everyday situations) in order to justify their pre-supposed theory. Then they have to evade the obvious conclusions that they are left with after they use faulty logic, as shown above. In all of the above examples, the children are included in their parents. It is because of the parents that infants can be Americans, hotel guests, Romanians, blessed by Jesus, ride on a bus, etc. In all these examples, they are called the same thing as the parents, they are treated the same way as the parents, they are given the same protections as the parents, and they are given the same privileges as the parents. Only in the Credobaptist church are they treated as completely separate entities, who first need to mature into adults before they make vows on their own to be a Nazirite.

BORN CHRISTIANS?

With one united voice, all Credobaptists make the claim that a person does not inherit his Christianity from his parents. They belabor the point that "nobody is born a Christian." Even some in the Presbyterian and Reformed world subscribe to that silliness. (No wonder they can't put together a persuasive argument.) It's just as silly to argue that my children are not born with my last name, or that they are not born Americans. My children are Christians from birth, just like they are Americans from birth. The problem many of our Reformed Baptist brethren is that they confuse "Christian" with being "ordained unto eternal salvation." Those are two *very separate things*.

I think you would agree that there is a covenant community called the Church, and that there is a spiritual community called the elect, which is included in the former, but not vice versa.[1] We know the one; we don't know the other. This is a Scriptural norm. Israel was made up of many whose circumcision was not of the "heart," yet that did not remove them from the outward people known as Israel. They could completely reject Jehovah, and yet He did not hesitate to call them "his people" (Jer. 2:13). They were born into the Church. That hasn't changed. Gentile Christians have been brought into the "commonwealth of Israel" (Eph. 2:11-13). We are a "holy nation," a "special people," etc. We are a covenant community made up of elect and non-elect. And just like Israel, our children are born into it. That's not to say that they are born "elect" in the salvific sense; nobody knows that. But they are born "Christians." It was the heathen who first gave the name *Christian* to the disciples of Christ; so ask any heathen, and they will call your family a "Christian family." If the Credobaptist can get that one point, his protests against infant baptism will evaporate. "Christians" are "disciples" of Christ. Credobaptists are stuck on "true disciples," the "elect," and the "new birth," as qualifications to make one a "true Christian." But the Bible uses the term "Christian" for anyone in the covenant community, regardless of their election status. Jesus said that you can be His "disciple indeed," but He did not insinuate that the other disciples were not disciples; they were just bad disciples.

> From that time many of His disciples went back and walked with Him no more (John 6:66).

---

[1] *Reformed* Baptists will certainly agree with this, but those of the Arminian persuasion may not. The point that I'm making is still the same, even to someone who is an Arminian: my children are Christians until they reject Christianity.

You see? *Many* of His *disciples* walked away from Him, just as many of His *disciples* today still walk away. But they are all still called "disciples" prior to their abandonment of said discipleship. This is equivalent to an Old Testament discussion of circumcision of the heart. Perhaps the disciple will turn his back on Christ one day, but that is irrelevant to the present decision of whether or not to baptize him. Peter did not bemoan the fact that Ananias and Sapphira had been baptized, but he knew that their baptism made their judgment that much more severe. They were called "believers." They were baptized. Their belief was false. Their baptism was true. Thus, their judgment is worse. A disciple is a learner, and nothing more. All learners of Jesus Christ are to be baptized per Matthew 28.

So to be more specific, can our children be born into a state of discipleship? Can the parents make that decision for them? Well, of course they can; just like a Levite was born into a state of service to the temple, a priest was born into a state of service to the people, and a Nazirite was born into a state of service to God. They were all proclaimed to be such by God Himself (Num. 3:39; Ex. 27:21; Jud. 13:15).

And in the case of the Levites, God made their state of service perpetual; each generation of the line of Levi was born into a state of service to God and His tabernacle/temple. Was God wrong for doing so? God didn't care that some of the Levites rebelled; they were still set apart to Him, and it only made the rebels' judgment that much more severe. So if a newborn child, apart from any act of his own will, can be put on a path of service to God, the temple, and the Church; how can anyone say that the child cannot also be put on a path of discipleship to Jesus Christ? God applauded Abraham for doing this very thing! (Gen. 18:19) Each one of those examples was a learner of the path he was put on at birth. He was a disciple of Christ. Was a Levite not really a Levite until he surrendered his will to the path he was born into? Was Samson not a "true" Nazirite until he surrendered his will to the path he was born into? Their will did one of two things; either it rejected the path they were already put into, or it embraced the path they were put into. Either way, they were already born into a certain state which they later had to embrace or reject. They were born into that state because of their parents. The state our children are born into is the state of a Christian—a disciple of Christ. They are born into it; and they need to be baptized per God's command, whether they reject it later or not.

Furthermore, my name is Andrew Camp. Will anyone argue that my child is not born into a state of being a "Camp," simply because he has not chosen it with his own free will? You certainly know that when my child is grown, he could reject my family and my family name if he so chooses, due to his hatred of us. But he would have to reject it, because he is already in that state. If there were a sign given to all Camps, I would not hesitate to give it to an adopted 13-year-old or my newborn children, regardless of the fact that they could later reject being a Camp.

I have a good Reformed Baptist friend, who had just gotten his US citizenship. He is originally from Ecuador. When he was expecting his first child, I asked him if he knew what his vow of citizenship did for his unborn child. He looked at me, perplexed; and I told him, "You have made every one of your future children citizens of the USA, by virtue of their being *your* children. They will be born US citizens automatically, because their father is a US citizen." Then I told him that the only "nation" on earth that refuses citizenship to the children of its citizens, is the Credobaptist Church of Jesus Christ—a "holy nation" that refuses citizenship to its children.

In the Old Testament, everyone was very proud of their birth; even the Apostle Paul "boasts" of it.[1] Why? Because they knew that God dealt in a special way with those born into certain families. It didn't mean that they were eternally elect, by any means (although some mistakenly thought that it did). But it certainly meant that God dealt with the children of an Israelite differently than He dealt with a child of a Philistine. As Paul points out, "to them were given the

---

[1] Philippians 3:5.

oracles of God." They were different. That hasn't changed. When Rahab got saved, her family was suddenly treated differently by God (Josh. 6:17, 23, 25). That didn't make them eternally saved,[1] but it did make them different. They were included in God's community. When the Philippian jailer got saved, it was the same way; his family suddenly became different. That didn't mean that they were all saved; it meant that they were different. They were in God's community, and they were all baptized.

So I ask you, "Why does birth no longer count for anything?" How are my children different from the Israelite children? Why can my children no longer be proud of their heritage? Why must they be individualistic, and reject the fact that by the grace of God, they were born into a Christian home? Why must we tell them that they are on no better footing than the heathen? It's simply not true. The Christian has many more privileges; and therefore, he carries a much bigger burden. Our children should be proud of the fact that God cared for them, and placed them in a God-honoring home to learn His Word and be kept from the world, simply because He loved their parents.[2] We can't lose sight of that fact. The only reason Jesus loved us enough to die for us, was that God the Father gave us to Him.[3] His love for us is only a reflection of the love He has for the Father.

Remember that the family is another institution that God made to reflect what He already experiences. When you love your son and care for him more than you do the heathen children, that is a God-given love. To think that it's different would be like thinking that God loves us enough to send his Son to die for us, but then tells us, "Nope, the children that you yourself love and would die for, are not included in My people until they decide for themselves." That is rank Arminianism. The entire Baptist system is Arminian, which is why we always say that "Reformed Baptist" is a contradiction in terms.

We and our children only need to remember, like the Israelites of old, that our heritage is by no means a ticket to heaven. It's a

---

[1] Spiritually speaking, of course; because they were certainly saved physically.
[2] Deuteronomy 4:37.
[3] John 17:6.

blessing from God, but we are never to presume on that heritage as if *it* is our Christ (1 Cor. 10).

A man once told me, "Discipleship in Christianity is an issue of willful and public submission, not something that we earn based on our birth." Can you imagine someone saying this to a Levite? "Discipleship to Jehovah is an issue of willful and public submission, not something we earn based on our birth." Of course, every Levite was a Levite by birth, and was proclaimed by God to be one of His servants before he was born. He inherited this status of a "servant" by virtue of being born to Levite parents. So did every Israelite, for that matter. Every Israelite was automatically a disciple of Jehovah *by birth!*[1]

So, considering the fact that Levites are Levites *from birth,* do you think that when all the Levites are consecrated in Numbers 8:5-7, the infants might have been there as well?[2] I don't see why not; if so, then infants were sprinkled along with all the adults. Hmmm...sounds familiar.

---

[1] Please notice that the Bible stresses that even *infant* Levites were considered Levites...

"Number the children of Levi after the house of their fathers, by their families: every male from a month old and upward shalt thou number them" (Num. 3:15).

"Those that were numbered of them, according to the number of all the males, from a month old and upward, even those that were numbered of them were seven thousand and five hundred" (Num. 3:22).

"In the number of all the males, from a month old and upward, were eight thousand and six hundred, keeping the charge of the sanctuary" (Num. 3:28).

"And those that were numbered of them, according to the number of all the males, from a month old and upward, were six thousand and two hundred" (Num. 3:34).

"All that were numbered of the Levites, which Moses and Aaron numbered at the commandment of the LORD, throughout their families, all the males from a month old and upward, were twenty and two thousand" (Num. 3:39).

[2] And the LORD spake unto Moses, saying, "Take the Levites from among the children of Israel, and cleanse them. And thus shalt thou do unto them, to cleanse them: Sprinkle water of purifying upon them, and let them shave all their flesh, and let them wash their clothes, and so make themselves clean" (Num. 8:5-7).

What about the Kohathites? There were three sons of Levi, whose descendants were numbered by Moses and set apart for the work of the tabernacle: Gershon, Kohath, and Merari. Each family had a particular duty in regard to the tabernacle work. And each male person in that family was assigned that particular duty *at birth*. Each family had the males numbered from one month old and up (Num. 3:22, 28, 34) and the duties were assigned to them all (Num. 3:25, 28, 36). The clearest example that the infants were included, is found in Numbers 3:28:

> According to the number of all the males, **from a month old and above**, there were eight thousand six hundred **keeping charge of the sanctuary.**

A one-month-old child "keeping charge of the sanctuary"? Really? How can that be? A Kohathite parent could look at his child and declare that his child *was* a "keeper of the sanctuary"; not *was in training to be*, or someday *would be*, or even *could be*. His child was a keeper of the sanctuary. In his infancy, he had the same status as the adult Kohathites; he was a Kohathite. He could not carry any of the sanctuary items yet, but that did not mean that he was not a Kohathite who was a "keeper of the sanctuary." On the contrary, he was a Kohathite who was now learning how to perform the duties that had already been assigned to him. He was not in the hopes of someday being a Kohathite; he was one now, as an infant. If he hated his duties when he got older, he could reject his heritage and leave Israel. But there was no magical time when the infant suddenly became a Kohathite; rather, he was born as one. Well, the same can be said of our children. They are born Christians with all of the duties of Christians. No, they can't believe yet, or love their brethren yet, or do any other duties that Christians have. But they are being trained to do the duties that are already assigned to them. Once again, this is a Biblical norm.

The Word βαπτίζω

Our Credobaptist brethren make a big deal out of the meaning of the word βαπτίζω. Of course, they have to, because they don't have much else. They want us all to interpret the word according to its strict lexical meaning, which they tell us is *immerse,* of course. Never mind that their own Bible translations don't translate it as they say it should be.[1] And never mind that all lexicons have alternative meanings for the word. That's beside the point. They still maintain that it means *immerse,* and nothing but *immerse.* To the contrary of what they assert, βαπτίζω does not exclusively mean *immerse,* as you can see if you pick up any Greek lexicon. Notice the following meanings given by these sources.

Thayer's Greek-English Lexicon of the New Testament:
1) to dip repeatedly, to immerse, to submerge (of vessels sunk)
2) to cleanse by dipping or submerging, **to wash, to make clean with water, to wash one's self, bathe**
3) to overwhelm

Strong's Exhaustive Concordance:
... (in the New Testament) **of ceremonial** *ablution,* especially (technically) of the ordinance of Christian *baptism:* - baptist, baptize, **wash.**

A Greek English Lexicon of the New Testament, Bauer:
..."dip, immerse, dip oneself, **wash** (in non-Christian lit. also 'plunge, sink, drench, overwhelm', etc.), in our lit. only in ritual sense"...

---

[1] Some people actually did try it once, and it wasn't very popular because it sounded ridiculous. Some examples will be provided later in this section. This translation was called the American Bible Union Version. In my opinion, all Credobaptists should be using that version of the Bible, if they were consistent. But as we have seen, they are not.

So we can see that a legitimate translation of the word βαπτίζω is "to make clean with water," "to wash one's self," "ceremonial ablution," or just plain "wash." Contrary to so many Credobaptist complaints, I know of no Paedobaptist who claims that the word βαπτίζω means *sprinkle*. But the mode of sprinkling can very easily be employed to "make clean with water" or "to wash one's self." I do it every day. In the King James Version, βαπτίζω is translated "wash" five times,[1] with all other occurrences being transliterated. It is never once translated as *immerse*. Why do you think the translators chose not to just translate it as *immerse*? We'll see why soon.

Now, there are volumes of books written just on the meaning of that *one word*. In particular, James W. Dale wrote four volumes, all on the usage of that *one word*. He examines the usage of that word in the Bible and every other ancient Greek source, almost exhaustively. They are amazing volumes, and I recommend them to anyone making an in-depth study of the issue. They would never have been written if it were not for the fact that Credobaptists make the claim that the word only means one thing. That being said, Dale's books are good reading, but are not really necessary. I'm glad Dale wrote them so we can refer to them when needed, but it's not really that difficult to explain to a typical Credobaptist.

The contention of all the Bible translators and the Paedobaptist churches is that the word βαπτίζω took on a ceremonial meaning. This is easy to demonstrate, and it's not the only word that this happened to.[2] Look up the definition of "supper" (Greek: δεῖπνον)

---

[1] Mark 7:4 (twice); Mark 7:8; Luke 11:38; Hebrews 9:10.

[2] The Credobaptists' own use of the term *baptism* proves my point here. Notice how Credobaptists tell us that we must be "*baptized* by immersion." They don't say that "you must be *immersed* by immersion"; but rather, that you must be "*baptized* by immersion." If *baptism* means *immersion,* then you would expect them to just say, "You must be immersed." But they don't. They use the first term (*baptism*) ceremonially, and the second term (*immersion*) descriptively. They are stating that there is a ceremony that must take place, and that ceremony is to be done by the mode of immersion. Well, the Jews and early Christians did the same thing—they used the word *baptism* ceremonially. But unlike our Credobaptist brethren, they

in a dictionary or Greek lexicon, and show it to the Credobaptist. It will say, "an evening meal." Then ask the Credobaptist why they celebrate the Lord's Supper in the morning or afternoon? Why don't they do it in the evening, as the word imports? And why isn't it a full meal? The word imports that as well. The answer, of course, is because the word has taken on a ceremonial meaning. So when we refer to the "Supper," we all know that we mean a small cup of juice (or wine, for Presbyterians!) and a crumb of bread. You can think of other words that have had their meanings changed as well. One word that is very much to the point is "bath." When we tell people, "Take a bath," we certainly don't care if they take a shower. The word is used synonymously with any method of cleaning yourself. The same thing happened with βαπτίζω. It came to be synonymous with "cleanse" or "purify."[1] This is why all of our Bibles also translate it as "wash."

So why did the translators of the Bible tend to transliterate the word βαπτίζω instead of translating it?[2] Are all the translators evil Paedobaptists, trying to spread their false doctrine? Or do they actually have some grammatical reasons for transliterating it? Wouldn't you think something was wrong if you were reading

---

never stated the mode. They never said, "You must be baptized by...(mode)"; they only said, "You must be baptized." They assumed that you knew how the ceremony of baptism was performed.

[1] John 3:25.

[2] The famous Credobaptist theologian John Gill spoke about this. "Had our translators, instead of adopting the Greek word *baptize* in all places where the ordinance of baptism is made mention of, truly translated it, and not have left it untranslated, as they have, the controversy about the manner of baptizing would have been at an end, or rather have been prevented; had they used the word *dip*, instead of *baptize*, as they should have done, there would have been no room for a question about it." John Gill, Body of Divinity pg 910.

Perhaps if Mr. Gill had lived to see the version of Scripture he wanted, he would have changed his mind, like all of the other Credobaptists who rejected the American Bible Union Version. Not to mention the fact that "dip" is not a valid translation of the word βαπτίζω.

something that said, "Andrew came soaking in the house"? You would think that something was left out, and I forgot a word. As it stands, the statement doesn't make any sense, and it leaves you with more questions than answers. What do you mean by *soaking*? Soaking with or in what? How are you soaking? What is the object that you are soaking? We don't use verbs like that in any language. Verbs like that must be qualified to make them intelligible, like this: "Andrew came soaking his kids with a squirt gun." Well, that's the same problem we would have in many of the texts, if we translated the word βαπτίζω instead of transliterating it. That is why the translators wisely understood it to have taken on a ceremonial meaning; and they transliterated the word in places where a translation didn't make sense to them.

A single example will suffice. If we translated the word βαπτίζω as *immerse,* rather than transliterating it as *baptism,* then Mark 1:4 would say, "John came **immersing** in the wilderness, and preaching the **immersion** of repentance unto remission of sins." The question would come up, *"What* exactly was he immersing? And *into* what was he immersing?" The wilderness? Really? You see, verbs are not used that way. In order to be understood, they need to be qualified. Yes, if we read on, we could come to a contextual understanding; but it surely makes that sentence sound ridiculous. That is why the translators understood that the word must have taken on a ceremonial meaning, and should thus be transliterated rather than translated. Please notice that even if it were translated as *wash,* it would still sound silly. "John came washing in the wilderness" is equally hard to understand. So it's not an issue of what word was used to translate; it's an issue of translating the word *at all.* The translators were wise.

As I've pointed out, every time the Bible translators felt like the word needed to be translated rather than transliterated, they used the translation *wash.* Did they do so wrongly? Let's take a look at some Biblical texts to see if it makes sense to translate βαπτίζω as *immerse.* It may surprise you to learn that it has been tried. Some over-zealous Credobaptists were so convinced that they were correct in their theory, that they made an immersionist version. It's called the American Bible Union Version, and it's pretty bad. (This version is not in use anymore by any Baptist church that I know of.) They stay consistent and translate the word βαπτίζω only as *immerse*. It reads just like my example on Mark 1:4 above: badly. But on the other hand, if you took the exact same texts in which the translators chose to transliterate βαπτίζω as "baptism"; and instead of transliterating the word, we translate it according to what Paedobaptists have been saying for two millennia—that is, to ceremonially cleanse or purify; the verses make perfect sense. Now, I do not advocate translating it this way; I'm perfectly happy with the transliteration of *baptism*. It's just impressive to see how silly it sounds to translate the word as *immerse,* when the other equally legitimate translation of *ceremonially cleanse* or *ceremonially purify* renders it perfectly understandable. But don't take my word for it. Read it for yourself, and see how utterly ridiculous this debate becomes when someone will only allow one meaning of a word. Read the texts below in the New King James Version, the American Bible Union Version, and my own "Paedobaptist version"; and see which makes more sense.

Mark 1:4

NKJV: John came **baptizing** in the wilderness and preaching a **baptism** of repentance for the remission of sins.

ABUV: John came **immersing** in the wilderness, and preaching the **immersion** of repentance unto remission of sins.

My version: John came **ceremonially purifying** in the wilderness and preaching a **ceremonial purification** of repentance for the remission of sins.

Mark 7:4

NKJV: When they come from the marketplace, they do not eat **unless they wash.** And there are many other things which they have received and hold, like the **washing** of cups, pitchers, copper vessels, and couches.

ABUV: And coming from the market, **except they immerse themselves,** they do not eat. And there are many other things which they received to hold, **immersions** of cups, and pots, and brazen vessels, and couches.

My version: When they come from the marketplace, they do not eat **unless they ceremonially purify themselves.** And there are many other things which they have received and hold, like the **ceremonial purifying** of cups, pitchers, copper vessels, and couches

Mark 16:16

NKJV: He who believes and is **baptized** will be saved; but he who does not believe will be condemned.

ABUV: He that believes and is **immersed** shall be saved; but he that believes not shall be condemned.

My version: He who believes and is **purified** will be saved; but he who does not believe will be condemned.

Matthew 28:19

NKJV: Go therefore and make disciples of all the nations, **baptizing** them in the name of the Father and of the Son and of the Holy Spirit.

ABUV: Go therefore, and disciple all the nations, **immersing** them in the name of the Father, and of the Son, and of the Holy Spirit.

My version: Go therefore and make disciples of all the nations, **ceremonially purifying** them in the name of the Father and of the Son and of the Holy Spirit.

Luke 7:29, 30

NKJV: And when all the people heard Him, even the tax collectors justified God, having been **baptized** with the **baptism** of John. But the Pharisees and lawyers rejected the will of God for themselves, not having been **baptized** by him.

ABUV: And all the people, hearing it, and the publicans, justified God, having been **immersed** with John's **immersion**. But the Pharisees and the lawyers rejected the counsel of God toward themselves, not having been **immersed** by him.

My version: And when all the people heard Him, even the tax collectors justified God, having been **ceremonially purified** with the **ceremonial purification** of John. But the Pharisees and lawyers rejected the will of God for themselves, not having been **ceremonially purified** by him.

Luke 11:37-39

NKJV: And as He spoke, a certain Pharisee asked Him to dine with him. So He went in and sat down to eat. When the Pharisee saw it, he marveled that He had not first **washed** before dinner. Then the Lord said to him, "Now you Pharisees make the outside of the cup and dish clean, but your inward part is full of greed and wickedness.

ABUV: And as he was speaking, a Pharisee asked him to dine with him and he went in, and reclined at table. And the Pharisee, seeing it, wondered that he did not first **immerse himself** before dinner. And the Lord said to him: Now ye Pharisees cleanse the outside of the cup and the platter; but your inward part is full of rapacity and wickedness.

My version: And as He spoke, a certain Pharisee asked Him to dine with him. So He went in and sat down to eat. When the Pharisee saw it, he marveled that He had not first **ceremonially purified himself** before dinner. Then the Lord said to him, "Now you Pharisees make the outside of the cup and dish clean, but your inward part is full of greed and wickedness.

Of course, in all of the examples above that are marked as "My version," I have only taken the New King James Version text and inserted "ceremonially purify" in the appropriate place.[1] (Don't be confused; I'm not really writing my own version.) These texts have been pointed out for hundreds of years to the Credobaptist community, and I have observed two responses. To the average Credobaptist attending a Credobaptist church, these examples will make an impression. They will be stunned. I had one man get mad once, and say, "Why didn't anyone ever tell me this before?" But the scholars, on the other hand, are those whose job is to defend this position. They will answer like Alexander Carson, the much-lauded Credobaptist apologist from the 19th century...

"Now I will ... still contend that there is nothing like *an absurdity* in the supposition that the *couches* were immersed. The thing is quite possible, and who will say that the superstitious Pharisees might not practise it? It would indeed be a very inconvenient thing, but what obstacles will not superstition overcome? It would be a foolish thing; but who would expect anything but folly in will-worship? Such religious practice was indeed absurd, but it is an abuse of language to assert that it is *an absurdity* to say that the Pharisees immersed their couches."[2]

Yes, Alexander Carson was a grown man, and he still argued that way. "So what if they had to immerse their couches three times a day; so what if that means they were always sitting on wet furniture;

---

[1] *Purify* is a synonym for *baptize,* according to John 3.
[2] Alexander Carson. Baptism, It's Mode and Subjects. Pg 71.

so what if it was too big to make it practical to immerse; so what that they would have had to draw water from a well to fill a pool to immerse their couches in…three times a day. So what? It still happened, because it had to happen, in order to protect my theory!"

It is indeed doubtful that you will run into someone who is so extreme that they will admit what Mr. Carson does. And if you do run into someone like that, it may be best to turn and run; because for those people, you could have a text that said they baptized their tent daily, and he would still argue that they immersed it. To people of that level of persuasion, it doesn't matter how foolish it gets; their theory has to be defended.

"They all shall know me"?

Hebrews 8 records something that Reformed "Covenantal" Baptists obviously consider to be a cornerstone of their theory. (Another cornerstone is the Burial Theory, which we will discuss next. But if the Burial Theory is the cornerstone of their theory of "mode," then Jeremiah 31 is certainly the cornerstone of their theory of Church membership.) Jeremiah prophesied about the "New Covenant"; and the Apostle, in the book of Hebrews, quotes him directly, referring to our current-day New Covenant circumstances.

> Behold, the days are coming, says the LORD, when I will make a new covenant with the house of Israel and with the house of Judah—not according to the covenant that I made with their fathers in the day that I took them by the hand to lead them out of the land of Egypt, My covenant which they broke, though I was a husband to them, says the LORD. But this is the covenant that I will make with the house of Israel after those days, says the LORD: I will put My law in their minds, and write it on their hearts; and I will be their God, and they shall be My people. No more shall every man teach his neighbor, and every man his brother, saying, 'Know the LORD,' for **they all shall**

know Me, from the least of them to the greatest of them, says the LORD. For I will forgive their iniquity, and their sin I will remember no more (Jer. 31:31-34).

The Credobaptist contention is that our babies can't know the Lord in any cognitive sense, so they are not included in the New Covenant like they were in the Old Covenant. They tell us that this is the "new" part of the New Covenant.[1] Oh my! There are so many things wrong with that statement that it is hard to know where to start. If you point out that there are persons in their Credobaptist church who do not "know the Lord" in a salvific sense, they will only reply that those persons are not "truly" in the New Covenant. So what is a Paedobaptist to do?

Well, a few things can be said. First, point out that if they are going to take the prophecy wooden-literally, then they must, of necessity, hold to Replacement Theology. This is because it is "Israel" that is said to be "My people."[2] I am certainly all right with that, but some Baptists are not. Whether or not this will be an issue, depends upon the brand of Credobaptist that you are dealing with. So let's suppose the Credobaptist *is* all right with that, and he admits that the Church is the "Israel" that was prophesied…what then? Regardless of his view on Replacement Theology, ask him about the original hearers of the prophecy. Whether or not you believe that "Israel" in this prophecy is meant to be understood as Israel of the flesh or Israel as the Church, we can at least agree that Jeremiah's intended hearers were the Israelites he was speaking to. Can you imagine a faithful Jewish man going home to his family, and telling them, "Well, I heard that beloved prophet Jeremiah talking today about our upcoming captivity. And I have wonderful news! He said that once we get back from captivity, our children will no longer be in Jehovah's covenant people. What a blessing! He is going to remove these unbelieving infants from His people, and make them prove themselves before they can claim the name of an Israelite!" Do you think it would even

---

[1] See the discussion in "A Reformed Baptist Manifesto" by Samuel Waldron page 70.

[2] See section in Chapter 4 titled "Is Israel the Church?"

be possible that a Jew would have understood Jeremiah's prophecy to mean that? I think it's safe to say that you will probably never run into a Credobaptist that would be willing to answer that question in the affirmative. So press this point home. It's impossible that a faithful Jew could have understood Jeremiah's prophecy to exclude children; because the "My people" being addressed by Jeremiah, included the children. Every time the Lord specified "My people," He *always* included the children.[1]

Now, let's go farther. Take them to another prophecy that is quoted in the New Testament.

> And it shall come to pass afterward That I will pour out My Spirit **on all flesh**; Your sons and your daughters shall prophesy, Your old men shall dream dreams, Your young men shall see visions. And also on My menservants and on My maidservants I will pour out My Spirit in those days (Joel 2:28, 29).

Of course, this is quoted by the Apostle Peter on the day of Pentecost. The Holy Spirit had just fallen upon the Apostles, and they began to speak in tongues and to prophesy. Then the inspired Apostle tells those persons who are accusing them of being drunk, that what they were witnessing was actually the fulfillment of Joel's prophecy. The inspired Apostle just took a prophecy about "all flesh," and applied it to an occurrence that by no means applied to "all flesh." Was the inspired Apostle wrong? Of course not. But the Apostle Peter had no problem with the ultimate language of the prophecy "all flesh" being applicable to the very near and non-ultimate circumstances they were currently experiencing. In a certain sense, "all flesh" could be taken as literally fulfilled; that is, in the sense of people from all over the known world being assembled there, to have the Spirit poured out upon them. But according to the Credobaptist principle that they use with the prophecy of Jeremiah,

---

[1] See the section in Chapter 4 titled "Are they God's people?"

this prophecy of Joel should mean that every person in the world had the Holy Spirit poured out upon them. That, of course, would be an error, just like the one that they make with the New Covenant prophecy in Jeremiah 31.[1] Just like with Joel, there is a certain sense in which "they shall all know Me" is true; but not in the wooden-literal sense that Credobaptists take it to mean. If "they shall all know Me" is to be taken in the sense that our Credobaptist brethren want to take it in, then we should rule out witnessing; because we are no longer supposed to say to our "neighbor," "Know the Lord."

Obviously the Apostle is using Jeremiah 31 just like Peter used Joel 2. They really did point to the fulfillment of what the Apostles pointed them to. But just like the prophecy of Joel, which can only be ultimately fulfilled when all men are Christians and literally have "all flesh" filled with the Holy Spirit; so also, the ultimate fulfillment of Jeremiah 31 is only in the eternal state. Witnessing will no longer be needed in that time. Prophecy is not to be interpreted in a

---

[1] For additional references to prove this point, you can look at the following: "As it is written in the book of the words of Isaiah the prophet, saying: "THE VOICE OF ONE CRYING IN THE WILDERNESS: 'PREPARE THE WAY OF THE LORD; MAKE HIS PATHS STRAIGHT. EVERY VALLEY SHALL BE FILLED AND EVERY MOUNTAIN AND HILL BROUGHT LOW; THE CROOKED PLACES SHALL BE MADE STRAIGHT AND THE ROUGH WAYS SMOOTH; AND ALL FLESH SHALL SEE THE SALVATION OF GOD'" (Luke 3:4-6).

"BEHOLD! MY SERVANT WHOM I HAVE CHOSEN, MY BELOVED IN WHOM MY SOUL IS WELL PLEASED! I WILL PUT MY SPIRIT UPON HIM, AND HE WILL DECLARE JUSTICE TO THE GENTILES. HE WILL NOT QUARREL NOR CRY OUT, NOR WILL ANYONE HEAR HIS VOICE IN THE STREETS. A BRUISED REED HE WILL NOT BREAK, AND SMOKING FLAX HE WILL NOT QUENCH, TILL HE SENDS FORTH JUSTICE TO VICTORY; AND IN HIS NAME GENTILES WILL TRUST" (Matt. 12:18-21).

But I say, have they not heard? Yes indeed: "THEIR SOUND HAS GONE OUT TO ALL THE EARTH, AND THEIR WORDS TO THE ENDS OF THE WORLD" (Rom. 10:18).

Really? Did no one *ever* hear Jesus' voice in the streets? There are places on this planet where men have not set foot, let alone Christian men preaching the Gospel. This doesn't mean the prophecies were wrong. But we would interpret them incorrectly if we took them wooden-literally.

wooden-literal way, like you would interpret a didactic portion of Scripture. Many times, prophecy uses apocalyptic language that cannot be interpreted in the way that our Credobaptist brethren want to, like with Jeremiah 31. So, coupled with the fact that we still do, in fact, say to our neighbor, "Know the Lord"; I suggest that this passage is not making the point that our Credobaptist brethren wish it to make. But my suggestion doesn't really carry weight, does it? So let me prove it to you from Scripture.

Please keep in mind that it's not just prophecy that must be interpreted carefully. Scripture uses this type of ultimate language in many different scenarios. Notice what the Scripture says about Simon the sorcerer.

> But there was a certain man called Simon, who previously practiced sorcery in the city and astonished the people of Samaria, claiming that he was someone great, to whom **they all gave heed, from the least to the greatest**, saying, "This man is the great power of God" (Acts 8:9, 10).

Are we to believe that every man, woman, and child fell for his sorcerous tricks? No, of course not. Aren't we supposed to believe from this that the *vast majority* of Samaritans believed that Simon was "the great power of God"? Are we to suppose that *not one* of the Samaritans was skeptical of Simon's sorcery? After all, there were a lot of people in Samaria, many of whom had just converted to Christianity under the preaching of Philip. And what about our Lord's ministry to Samaria? The woman at the well was a true convert, as well as many others whom she preached to.

> And **many of the Samaritans of that city believed in Him** because of the word of the woman who testified, "He told me all that I ever did." So when the Samaritans had come to Him, they urged Him to stay with them; and He stayed there two days. And **many more believed** because of His own word. Then they said to the woman,

"Now we believe, not because of what you said, for we ourselves have heard Him and **we know that this is indeed the Christ, the Savior of the world"** (John 4:39-42).

Those look like true converts to me. But the exact same language of Acts 8 is used in Jeremiah 31. "All," "from the least to the greatest." And we see that, indeed, it was not "all" in a literal, ultimate sense in Acts 8; so are we really supposed to take it that way in Jeremiah 31? That will only be a reality in the eternal state.

Now here's my last point on this, and it's a dandy. Please read both passages from Jeremiah 31 and Acts 8 again, and notice the parallel that clearly exists between the two passages. And when you read them, remember that our Credobaptist brethren tell us that because infants cannot "know" the Lord, they cannot be included in His "people." Jeremiah 31 is the cornerstone of this argument of theirs. Now, let's take a look at that parallel.

Jeremiah 31: *My people...all shall know Me, from the least of them to the greatest of them.*

Baptist exposition:
Premise 1: "All" of the group called "My people," without exception, will know the Lord.
Premise 2: Infants cannot "know" the Lord.
Conclusion: Therefore, infants are not included in the group called "My people."

Acts 8: *The people of Samaria... all gave heed, from the least to the greatest.*

Baptist exposition:
Premise 1: "All" of the group called "the people of Samaria," without exception, "gave heed" to Simon the sorcerer.
Premise 2: Infants could not "give heed" to Simon.

Conclusion: Therefore, infants are not included in the group called "the people of Samaria."

I, for one, am not about to adopt the Credobaptist interpretation of those words. I think that when he is pressed, neither will the Credobaptist. Once again, the Credobaptist theory is found to be unbiblical and illogical. That horse is just plain dead.

So, I hate to beat a dead horse, but perhaps a study of Jeremiah's own language will be helpful. I mean, Baptists rely so heavily upon Jeremiah 31, that I would assume that someone must have looked to see how Jeremiah himself uses the terms "they shall all" and "from the least to the greatest." But I'm afraid that if there ever was a Baptist who did so, he must have ignored it; because he would come to the opposite conclusion of what he wants Jeremiah to mean. Notice:

> Therefore thus says the LORD of hosts, the God of Israel: "Behold, I will set My face against you for catastrophe and for cutting off all Judah. And I will take the remnant of Judah who have set their faces to go into the land of Egypt to dwell there, and **they shall all** be consumed and fall in the land of Egypt. They shall be consumed by the sword and by famine. They shall die, **from the least to the greatest,** by the sword and by famine; and they shall be an oath, an astonishment, a curse and a reproach!" (Jer. 44:11, 12)

Here we have Jeremiah speaking to the remnant of Judah, who are fleeing to Egypt for refuge. He clearly says that "they shall all" die while they are in Egypt, even "from the least to the greatest." Clear enough, huh? Based upon how the Baptists want us to interpret Jeremiah 31, we must assume that Jeremiah means "all," without exception. But is that what he means? Read on.

> For I will punish those who dwell in the land of Egypt, as I have punished Jerusalem, by the sword, by famine, and by pestilence, so

that **none of the remnant of Judah who have gone into the land of Egypt to dwell there shall escape or survive,** lest they return to the land of Judah, to which they desire to return and dwell. **For none shall return except those who escape** (Jer. 44:13, 14).

Wait a minute! If "all" were to die, "from the least to the greatest," how can there be an "except"? He goes on to state it again, by saying that "all the men of Judah who are in the land of Egypt shall be consumed by the sword and by famine, until there is an end to them" (Jer. 44:27). And in the very next sentence, he says, "Yet a small number who escape the sword shall return from the land of Egypt to the land of Judah; and all the remnant of Judah, who have gone to the land of Egypt to dwell there, shall know whose words will stand, Mine or theirs" (Jer. 44:28). Well, I guess if we were to interpret Jeremiah's words in the way Baptists do, then we would surely find out "whose words will stand." And they would *not be God's*. But we're not supposed to interpret Jeremiah's words like our Baptist brethren do. "All," "from the least to the greatest," does not mean "all," without exception.

The only other times when the phrase, "the least to the greatest," is used by Jeremiah, is when he says the following:

Because **from the least of them even to the greatest of them,** Everyone is given to covetousness; And from the prophet even to the priest, Everyone deals falsely (Jer. 6:13).

Therefore I will give their wives to others, And their fields to those who will inherit them; Because **from the least even to the greatest** Everyone is given to covetousness; From the prophet even to the priest Everyone deals falsely (Jer. 8:10).

Wow! "From the prophet even to the priest Everyone deals falsely"! Oh my! Well, what about the "prophet" who was speaking these words? Was Jeremiah "dealing falsely"? Or did he not mean those words in the sense that our Credobaptist brethren want us to believe they mean?

So challenge your Credobaptist brethren to examine how Jeremiah himself uses the very terms that they so adamantly demand must be interpreted to mean "all," without exception. Why does Jeremiah not think so? Once again, we should prefer the prophet's inspired understanding of those words, over our Credobaptist brethren's theory.

THE BURIAL THEORY

Just as we started this critique with a destruction of the Credobaptist *Magnus Opus* regarding the recipients of baptism, so also we end with their M*agnus Opus* regarding the mode of baptism—the so-called *Burial Theory*. I am perplexed as to how this has been used as the cornerstone of the immersionists' theory for so long. Some even take this to be the central argument for the Credobaptist position.[1] With no actual examples of administered immersions anywhere in the Bible, they are left with an imagined comparison of baptism to burial, in order to come up with anything that can support their theory.[2]

The following texts are used as support for the Burial Theory...

Or do you not know that as many of us as were baptized into Christ Jesus were baptized into His death? Therefore we were buried with Him by baptism into death, that just as Christ was raised from the dead by the glory of the Father, even so we also should walk in newness of life (Rom. 6:3, 4).

In Him you were also circumcised with the circumcision made without hands, by putting off the body of the sins of the flesh, by the circumcision of Christ, buried with Him in baptism, in which you also

---

[1] Carson pg 144.

[2] In the next chapter, I'll discuss what water represents, and how the Baptists have used this theory to render the Spirit-given meaning absurd.

were raised with Him through faith in the working of God, who raised Him from the dead (Col. 2:11, 12).

A typical Credobaptist sitting in his Credobaptist church, hearing a sermon on this theory, will be full of *Amen*'s and *Hallelujah*'s. From these two texts, the Credobaptists rest their case. Alexander Carson states:

"I value the evidence of these passages so highly, that I look on them as perfectly decisive."[1]

So once again, we must be ready to make people uncomfortable. Remember that this is a cornerstone of their theory; if this falls, the building ends up on the same crumbling heap of a theory that you have already left the Credobaptist with. So proceed with your brother by asking him to remember that the Burial Theory is a theory of *mode*. By this theory, the Credobaptists are trying to tell us that we can see the *mode* of baptism by what an *immersion* is supposedly picturing. According to the theory, we are supposed to see the *mode* clearly portrayed by what this passage is telling us that baptism does.

All right, let's play their game. Ask the Credobaptist, "Have you ever witnessed *an actual* burial?" If the mode of baptism is indeed supposed to be pictured *by burial* and resurrection, it would be much better pictured by the mode of *effusion* rather than by *immersion*. After all, what is the mode of *actual* burial? Has anyone ever witnessed someone being plunged into the dirt? On the contrary, the dirt is removed (or not), the person is put into the pit, and dirt is *thrown on top* of the deceased. As nobody on earth has ever actually witnessed a body being buried via plunging into the earth, and everyone who has ever witnessed *an actual burial* has seen dirt being *thrown on top* of the deceased; I must conclude that trying to prove the mode of immersion by using the Burial Theory is a product *of imagination,* not

---

[1] Carson pg 144.

empirical data.[1] However, using empirical data, we may conclude that *if* the Burial Theory has *any* merit at all, then we should baptize *by effusion*. After all, we don't get to just make up how someone gets buried, in order to fit our Credobaptist ideas, do we? A minister up to his waist in water, laying another person on his back beneath the water, *looks like no mode of burial anyone has ever witnessed on planet Earth.* Burial has always and forever been *by the mode of effusion.* You put the dirt ON the person. You can't get around it. Sorry, my Baptist friends. A better picture would be to put the baptized person in a bathtub, and turn on the shower or pour buckets of water on him. That, at least, would be an accurate picture of the proper mode of burial, and not the make-believe ceremony that they have somehow imagined to be a picture of burial. Then, once the person is immersed, they can pull him out to picture resurrection. Of course, they'll need to actually resurrect him, because he'll likely be drowned while waiting to be buried by the water.

Of course, Christ was not buried in the ground at all, either by immersion or effusion; He was *entombed.* That doesn't look like

---

[1] Wayne Grudem has apparently seen the defects in the Burial Theory, so he has changed the statement a little bit. He says: "The physical actions of going *down into* the water (where human beings cannot live for more than a few minutes) and coming *up out of* the water are so closely parallel to the actions of going down into the grave and coming up out of the grave that the connection is evident from the surface appearance of the actions, and no detailed explanation would be necessary." Systematic Theology pg 969 (Emphasis original)

Interestingly, Mr. Grudem needs to change his language away from the scriptural language of *burial,* in order to try to make sense of this theory. No longer is baptism a picture of *burial*, but now it's a picture of "going down into the grave." If he wants to contend that baptism pictures someone being lowered into a grave, I'll say that it is a fair representation—at least, that's the way it's portrayed by modern Baptists, by laying someone on their back. But *that's not burial;* and therefore, it has nothing to do with the only point of dispute. The burial happens *after* the body is lowered into the grave. Someone who has been lowered into a grave cannot be said to be buried until dirt is thrown over them. The Burial Theory is not about the mode of being lowered into the grave; rather, it's about the mode of *burial,* and thus, the *mode of baptism*—both of which are by effusion.

plunging. Maybe it would be better to put someone in a closet and then fling open the door! At least that would actually resemble the mode of Christ's burial and resurrection. The Christians in Rome (to whom the Epistle of Romans is addressed) would have seen the Romans cremating their dead. That certainly doesn't look like plunging. But alas, what is a Credobaptist to do? Could the Baptist actually try to do *baptism at sea*? Would a Baptist think that the Apostle Paul was thinking of a naval burial when he said those words? That, of course, would be the only burial in existence that would at least fit the plunging theme. But I think we all know that the Apostle was not thinking of that; and burial at sea is never anyone's preferred burial method—it's only a *necessary evil*.

You know, now that I think about it, perhaps I've misspoken. Yes, indeed, there *is* a burial recorded for us in the Bible, resembling a Credobaptist plunging. It's the only one I know of. Korah and his family suffered a plunging into the earth, which would look much like a person being "swallowed up" by the waters of the baptismal.

> Now it came to pass, as he finished speaking all these words, that the ground split apart under them, and the earth opened its mouth and **swallowed them up**, with their households and all the men with Korah, with all their goods (Num. 16:31, 32).

Let's see…God was the administrator…check; Korah was "plunged" into the earth…check; looks like it might help make the case for Baptists! Oh, but wait…this would also prove infant baptism, because his "household" went down with him; and in verse 27, it actually does say that there were "little children" in his household. Now what is a Credobaptist to do? Top it off with the fact that they were never drawn out of the ground to represent resurrection, and you're left with a pretty poor illustration.

Seriously, since Korah was suffering a distinct judgment of God, I don't think Baptists would want to use Korah as a precedent for their mode of baptism; even though it actually was an *administered immersion burial, which can be pictured by plunging into water.*

We can quickly close this section with two additional points. It's improper to say that these texts point in any way to the mode of baptism. They are telling us *what* the baptism did, not *how* it did it. Notice that the "baptism" in Romans 6:4 was *the means to* the "burial." So how does that make it a picture of the *mode* of burial? If I said that I was "buried with Christ by a shovel," would that mean that the shovel somehow has to be a picture of the mode of burial? No, it's simply the *tool* to *perform* that burial. Or what about Sodom and Gomorrah being buried by fire and brimstone? Is the fire and brimstone a picture of the mode of burial? So how do Credobaptists figure that baptism is a picture of burial?

> Therefore we were buried with Him *by* baptism into death (Rom. 6:4).

So the text is just telling us that we have been identified with Christ in all aspects of His life, death, and resurrection. Baptism is the tool by which that identification takes place. It was never meant to be a picture of any method of doing it.

Lastly, we can point out to the Credobaptist that if this text means that baptism is actually supposed to *look like* burial, then the exact same language in Galatians would mean baptism is supposed to *look like* the putting on of Christ...

> For as many of you as were baptized into Christ **have put on Christ** (Gal. 3:27).

How does someone "put on Christ"? Should it be pictured by putting on a robe? After all, if this language means what our Credobaptist brethren say it means, then we must admit that in some way, it pictorially resembles the putting on of Christ. How does plunging do that? I have an answer for you: it doesn't, because it's not a picture of putting on Christ, just as it's not a picture of being buried with Him. It's an actuality. We *really are* putting on Christ, and we *really are* being buried and raised with Christ; not pictorially, but *really*. Our baptism puts us into union with Christ. We are the "branches" in Christ.[1] In union with Him, we partake of His life, death, burial, resurrection, and reign. We partake of Christ and everything He is. This is why there is worse punishment for those who are partakers of Christ, and yet spurn His grace and trample the Son of God underfoot.[2]

There is more I could say about the Burial Theory; but at this point, you should be able to convince the average Credobaptist to have some level of doubt as to the truthfulness of the Credobaptist position. Now you can present a solid case for Paedobaptism by effusion; and after that, you can move on to discuss the minutia, which I discuss in Chapters 4 and following. With their presuppositions in question, you can show them that the rest of the Biblical data all makes sense in a Paedobaptist worldview. I can only conclude by saying that *the Burial Theory is dead and buried!*

---

[1] "I am the vine, you *are* the branches. He who abides in Me, and I in him, bears much fruit; for without Me you can do nothing" (John 15:5).

[2] "Of how much worse punishment, do you suppose, will he be thought worthy who has trampled the Son of God underfoot, counted the blood of the covenant by which he was sanctified a common thing, and insulted the Spirit of grace?" (Heb. 10:29)

Chapter 3

THE BIBLICAL BASIS FOR PAEDOBAPTISM BY SPRINKLING

Even if we destroyed the Credobaptist position, never to be revived again, it still wouldn't prove the Paedobaptist position by default. We must have a coherent Biblical basis upon which to build this position. This is what the Credobaptists claim that they are looking for from Paedobaptists; but in reality, they view each of your arguments through the lenses of their Baptistic theology. They need to have their first commitment destroyed—their glasses broken, so to speak; then they will be ready to have the Biblical case presented to them, and they can at least examine it with the broken Baptistic lenses that you left them with. Hopefully, Chapter 2 has given you a good start at doing just that. There are other issues and arguments (yet to be discussed in later chapters of this book) which I term the minutia of the debate. But for now, let's build the positive case for Paedobaptism by sprinkling; and then we will turn to the minutia of the debate.

Please allow me to first say a few words in regard to circumcision. For many years now, many of my Paedobaptist brethren have tied the justification for infant baptism to circumcision in the Old Covenant, and not without reason. I do not believe that their conclusions were completely in error, nor do I think that what they said is unprofitable to the discussion. I must part from them only when it comes to inseparably linking circumcision and baptism, and stating that the one *replaced* the other. Let me be very clear: there are very many good and clear parallels between circumcision and baptism, which are well worthy of discussion and debate; not the least of which is the initiatory aspect of the ordinances. But these are only parallels; baptism is not a "new circumcision." I think that our Paedobaptist brethren have erred by insisting that the one replaced the other, as if the one *foreshadowed* the other. Instead, what we need to stress is that *New Testament baptism* has replaced *Old Testament baptism*. While it is certainly true that New Testament baptism is the new sign of the covenant, and is, *in that sense,* a replacement for circumcision; we need to make it very clear that this does not in any way mean that circumcision somehow *foreshadowed* baptism. This just leads to confusion for the Credobaptists, and it leads to much useless chatter about the differences between the two, which we really have no interest in. Paedobaptists need to use the clear *parallels* between circumcision and baptism; and at the same time, they need to make it very clear that New Testament baptism did not *replace* Old Testament circumcision *as a new circumcision.* Rather, New Testament *baptism* replaced Old Testament *baptism.* In this chapter, we will prove this point; and we will build the argument for Paedobaptism by sprinkling, upon a more solid foundation.[1]

---

[1] Perhaps the reason why modern Paedobaptist apologists hold so tenaciously to this connection between circumcision and baptism, is because they are all tied to their confessions, which link the two inseparably. The confessions were written before the truly scholarly baptism debate began, during a day when theologians were much more concerned about the Lord's Supper. And while they did have the Anabaptists to contend with, the debate was not really taken seriously until the 18th and 19th centuries, when the Baptists shifted from their Bunyan-like charity to their Carson-like vehemence. This is when the baptism debate entered its apex. In Chapter 8, you will notice that the Anabaptist leader Menno Simons held to a theology of children that is closer to my perspective than to that of his followers today.

THE NATURE OF BAPTISM

Let's start with an exercise that I do with every Credobaptist I speak with. Our Credobaptist brethren are accustomed to pursuing rabbit-trails when they discuss this topic; so this exercise is meant to focus their thoughts, and to cut off some of those rabbit-trails right at the beginning of the discussion.

In the ordinance of baptism, we have to agree that there are at least three essentials: two parties and the element.

1. The *baptizer;* that is, the person physically performing the rite (the administrator)
2. The *baptized;* that is, the person upon whom or to whom the baptizer performs the rite
3. The *element;* that is, the water

If you do not have those three things, then you do not have Christian *baptism.* If our Credobaptist brethren would prefer to see a fourth item added to the list of essentials, such as...

4. The *mode;* that is, the immersion

...then, of course, you can ask him to show you a clear example, anywhere in the Bible, of one person immersing another person. He can't—unless, of course, that person is God, and then one great example could be given: the Flood. But since they will agree that without at least the first three, there is no baptism; then I will focus on those, as the disputed fourth item will collapse on its own.

So, with this in mind, let's look at Mark 1:4: "John came *baptizing* in the wilderness." John the Baptizer came *baptizing.* (There is one essential element.) Mark 1:5: "Then all...went out to him and were all *baptized* by him." People came to be *baptized.* (The second element.) Mark 1:8: "I baptized you *with water.*" John the Baptizer used *water*. (The third element of a proper baptism.) So now, when we are discussing exactly how John the Baptizer performed his baptisms, we should not forget all three of those elements. Did John the Baptizer take the baptized person and dunk him under the water, thus applying the baptized person to the element? Or did John the Baptizer take the element and apply it to the baptized person? This is an important question, is it not?

When God told John that He wanted him to go baptizing, do you think John knew exactly what he was supposed to do? After all, John was the son of a priest, and a descendant of Aaron. He was raised with the Word of God always before him; not only in word, but in picture as well, with all the ceremonies that he and his father observed and participated in. John knew the Old Testament well. So let's ask ourselves a question. Would John have just made up a mode of baptism on his own? Or do you think he would have been informed by the Word of God? According to Hebrews 9, the Old Testament is full of baptisms.

If we look in the Old Testament for examples of baptism, we need to remember the essentials. If those essentials are not there, then John would not have thought of that case as a precedent for the baptism he had to perform. So, was there anything in the Old Testament that included the three essential elements of baptism? As we scour the Old Testament for precedent baptisms, we need to be careful not to allow ourselves to get bogged down with every reference in the entire Old Testament to washing. It's not that they are unimportant washings; they are just irrelevant to the issue at hand. They were *self*-washings. If the washing does not have an administrator, a washed person, and the water; then we are not interested in it, because it doesn't fit the paradigm of Christian baptism.

In all of the God-inspired Old Testament Scriptures, I can find only five examples that include these three essentials to baptism. They are the **consecration of the people** at Sinai (Ex. 24:3-8; Heb. 9:19), the **consecration of the priests**, the **purification of the Levites**, the **purification of the lepers,** and the **purification of those who came in contact with a dead**

body (Numbers 19). In all five of those instances, we have a *performer of the right*, a person *having the right performed on him,* and the *element* applied by the performer. And of course, all five are by effusion.[1]

Of course, to our Credo brethren, the fact that they are performed by effusion rules out the idea that they should be referred to as "baptisms," because they add the fourth requirement as stated above. I understand that; but isn't it interesting that, in all of the Old Testament, there is not one example of one person dunking another person, and yet we have many instances of one person sprinkling another person. Of course, this is the true baptism. It was called baptism by the Jews of John's day, and it was performed daily in Israel, all the way up to the destruction of the temple in 70 AD. (More on this soon.)

CHRISTIAN BAPTISM: THE FULFILLMENT OF ALL OLD TESTAMENT BAPTISMS

The Lord's Supper was instituted during the Passover meal. Actually, it's not a new ordinance at all; it's a *changed* ordinance. It replaced all of the covenant meals of the Old Testament. It was taken from these other ordinances, such as the Passover, and given a new covenant meaning. It certainly has elements of the Old Testament covenant meals, but a new covenant meaning has been assigned to it. In this

---

[1] "The affusionist claims that no mode of ritual baptism is directly taught in the New Testament, but that as sprinkling, pouring, and laving were prescribed in the Old Testament for consecration and cleansing and as the Jews of Christ's day were accustomed only to such modes, it is most probably that these modes were brought forward into the new order. Had there been a change from the Old Testament requirement to a new mode for the church, it ought to have been indicated clearly." Chafer, Systematic Theology volume 7 pg 41.

same sense, baptism has come to us from the Old Testament baptisms. It's actually not a new ordinance at all; it's a *changed* ordinance. Baptism is instituted in place of all the Old Testament baptisms, and given a new covenantal meaning.

Our Christian baptism is an extension of the Old Testament baptisms that were commanded in the Law. That's right…baptism was commanded in the Law of Moses. In Hebrews 9:9, 10, we are told of the "symbolic" "fleshly ordinances," which were included in the tabernacle services. "Various baptisms" (διαφόροις βαπτισμοῖς) are said to be included in these ordinances. Do you think that John the Baptizer knew of these "various baptisms" that were required in the tabernacle services? After all, he was a priest's son. Paul goes on to compare the "baptisms" of the tabernacle services with the "sprinkling" of the blood of Jesus. (It's always sprinkling!) And included in these "baptisms," was the "sprinkling of the unclean." I suggest to you that this is the only baptism that the Bible knows, and no other. The form of New Testament baptism is sprinkling; and it all stems from the Old Testament "baptisms," which were, of course, purifications performed by *sprinkling.*

That passage in Hebrews hearkens back to Numbers 19, where we see the famous "red heifer" passage, and the subsequent use of the burnt red heifer ashes in the water of purification. The entire chapter is relevant, and the Paedobaptist apologist must be familiar with it.

> Now the LORD spoke to Moses and Aaron, saying, "This is the ordinance of the law which the LORD has commanded, saying: 'Speak to the children of Israel, that they bring you a red heifer without blemish, in which there is no defect and on which a yoke has never come. You shall give it to Eleazar the priest, that he may take it outside the camp, and it shall be slaughtered before him; and Eleazar the priest shall take some of its blood with his finger, and sprinkle some of its blood seven times directly in front of the tabernacle of meeting. Then the heifer shall be burned in his sight: its hide, its flesh, its blood, and its offal shall be burned. And the priest shall take cedar wood and hyssop and scarlet, and cast them into the midst of the fire burning

the heifer. Then the priest shall wash his clothes, he shall bathe in water, and afterward he shall come into the camp; the priest shall be unclean until evening. And the one who burns it shall wash his clothes in water, bathe in water, and shall be unclean until evening. **Then a man who is clean shall gather up the ashes of the heifer, and store them outside the camp in a clean place; and they shall be kept for the congregation of the children of Israel for the water of purification; it is for purifying from sin.** And the one who gathers the ashes of the heifer shall wash his clothes, and be unclean until evening. It shall be a statute forever to the children of Israel and to the stranger who dwells among them. He who touches the dead body of anyone shall be unclean seven days. **He shall purify himself with the water on the third day and on the seventh day; then he will be clean. But if he does not purify himself on the third day and on the seventh day, he will not be clean.** Whoever touches the body of anyone who has died, and does not purify himself, defiles the tabernacle of the LORD. **That person shall be cut off from Israel. He shall be unclean, because the water of purification was not sprinkled on him; his uncleanness is still on him. This is the law when a man dies in a tent:** All who come into the tent and all who are in the tent shall be unclean seven days; and every open vessel, which has no cover fastened on it, is unclean. Whoever in the open field touches one who is slain by a sword or who has died, or a bone of a man, or a grave, shall be unclean seven days. And for an unclean person they shall take some of the ashes of the heifer burnt for purification from sin, and running water shall be put on them in a vessel. **A clean person shall take hyssop and dip it in the water, sprinkle it on the tent, on all the vessels, on the persons who were there, or on the one who touched a bone, the slain, the dead, or a grave. The clean person shall sprinkle the unclean on the third day and on the seventh day;** and on the seventh day he shall purify himself, wash his clothes, and bathe in water; and at evening he shall be clean. **But the man who is unclean and does not purify himself, that person shall be cut off from among the assembly,** because he has defiled the sanctuary of the LORD. **The water of purification has not been sprinkled on him; he is**

unclean. It shall be a perpetual statute for them. He who sprinkles the water of purification shall wash his clothes; and he who touches the water of purification shall be unclean until evening. Whatever the unclean person touches shall be unclean; and the person who touches it shall be unclean until evening'"[1] (Num. 19:1-21).

There you have it—all three elements of baptism: a baptizer, a baptizee, and the element.

I have five points regarding this passage, and I think that they will show how it and the other Old Testament baptisms build the basis for New Testament baptism. These five points are proof of what we will call *Old Testament baptism*.

Point #1
This sprinkling of the water mixed with ashes was called *baptism* in both the Bible and the Septuagint.

Hebrews 9:7-14 tells us the Apostle's thoughts on the tabernacle services being typical of the work of Jesus Christ.

> But into the second part the high priest went alone once a year, not without blood, which he offered for himself and for the people's sins committed in ignorance; the Holy Spirit indicating this, that the way into the Holiest of All was not yet made manifest while the first tabernacle was still standing. *It was symbolic* for the present time in which both gifts and sacrifices are offered which cannot make him who performed the service perfect in regard to the conscience—

---

[1] Notice that if even one drop of the water of separation was sprinkled on the person, he was completely "clean." Our Credobaptist brethren have a hard time understanding this. In his *Body of Divinity,* John Gill quoting Maimon. in a positive fashion states: "What has a little water only sprinkled or poured on it, cannot be said to be washed" (pg 912). If that is true, then that which is plunged under water and immediately taken out again cannot be said to be "washed," either. But that is all irrelevant when we are talking about ceremonial purification. One drop of water is enough to cleanse all of the ceremonial filth off the dirtiest person—just like the blood of Christ.

concerned only with foods and drinks, *various washings (baptisms)*, and fleshly ordinances imposed until the time of reformation. But Christ came as High Priest of the good things to come, with the greater and more perfect tabernacle not made with hands, that is, not of this creation. Not with the blood of goats and calves, but with His own blood He entered the Most Holy Place once for all, having obtained eternal redemption. For if the blood of bulls and goats and *the ashes of a heifer, sprinkling the unclean, sanctifies for the purifying of the flesh,* how much more shall the blood of Christ, who through the eternal Spirit offered Himself without spot to God, cleanse your conscience from dead works to serve the living God? (Heb. 9:7-14)

The Apostle is clearly equating this "sprinkling the unclean" to the various "baptisms" that took place in the tabernacle services. But of course, a good Credobaptist is not going to take this sitting down. He may try to wiggle out of this in one of two ways. Let's quickly examine both in detail.

First, he may try to say that the "baptisms" that Paul is referring to are immersions in the Old Testament. This is answered in detail later, in Chapter 6, in a section entitled, "The Self-Washings." There, I will show that there *were no* immersions in the Old Testament, just as there are no immersions in the New Testament. But in addition to this point, the entire passage is detailing what the priests did in the *tabernacle services.* The only "washings" (baptisms) that the priest performed in the tabernacle services were *sprinklings.*[1] Have your

---

[1] Notice how John Gill tries to evade this clear truth by not keeping to the context of the tabernacle services. He says: "There were indeed divers washings, bathings, or baptisms, **under the legal dispensation**, for the purification of the persons and things unclean, by the ceremonial law; which had a doctrine in them, called the doctrine of baptisms, which taught the cleansing of the sin by the blood of Christ; but there was nothing similar in them to the ordinance of water-baptism, but immersion only." John Gill, Body of Divinity pg 897.

Well, the passage is speaking about the tabernacle services, not the "legal dispensation." Mr. Gill made the context broader in order to include things that he

friend read the context in Hebrews 9:1-10, in order to prove this fact. Then Paul goes on to detail these "baptisms" in the same passage, Hebrews 9:11-14. So if that objection comes up, go over this argument; and then, to seal the deal, ask him to point out where any priest in the tabernacle performed an immersion. (Cue the cricket noises.) There never was one.

Secondly, a Credobaptist may try to say that Paul's references to "baptism" are speaking of the Old Testament self-washings. The answer to this is the same as the first part of the previous paragraph. But in this case, please refer to the section on the self-washings, in Chapter 6, in which I show how none of them were performed by immersion.[1] And then, please refer to verse 20 of Numbers 19: "The water of purification has not been sprinkled on him; he is unclean." This proves that it was the sprinkling that was the administered purification. That is what rendered the person *clean*.

---

assumes were actually immersed. While I would be happy to engage in debate as to what, if anything, in the Bible was ever commanded to be *immersed in water*, I would first want to stick to the point, and have someone point out any immersion in the *tabernacle services*—which they could not do, of course.

Another attempt to evade the truth is made by Alexander Carson. Aside from the fact that he, too, did not restrict himself to the tabernacle services, he was sufficiently answered by James Dale: "But Dr. Carson would immerse the priests in the brazen sea (p. 444) – 'Such things as they offered for burnt offering, they washed in them (the lavers); but the sea was for the priests to wash in. Are not these immersions? Are not these different immersions even in the temple?' That is to say, he would make the priests to climb up over these "twelve oxen," and then climb up five cubits higher, and plunge into twenty thousand gallons of water to wash! How many times a day this was done; or, how many this water purified before it became impure, and had to be drawn off, and supplied with twenty thousand gallons of fresh water, we are not told." James W. Dale, Judaic Baptism pg. 179.

[1] Lest anyone should say that I believe that they *never* dunked themselves under water while bathing, I unequivocally state that, of course, someone *may* have done so in a lake they came upon. But it *could* not ever have been the *norm* until our modern day; and even now, it's not the norm.

The baptism of Numbers 19 is specifically called *baptism* (βαπτίζω) in the Septuagint also.[1] Notice this passage in Ecclesiasticus 31:25, 26[2]:

> He that washeth (baptizes) himself after the touching of a dead body, if he touch it again, what availeth his washing? So it is with a man that fasteth for his sins, and goeth again, and doeth the same: who will hear his prayer?

The writer of Ecclesiasticus clearly referred to this sprinkling as baptism. So now we know what the Jews thought that βαπτίζω meant, during the inter-testamental period. They saw a clean person (baptizer) sprinkling another person (baptized) with water mixed with ashes (element), as baptism. This is fascinating; and, as you'll see, the New Testament corroborates this wonderfully.

Now, if anyone attempts to evade this point by trying to say that the text says, "washeth himself," and therefore, it was by immersion; just refer them to verse 20 of Numbers 19: "But the man who is unclean and does not *purify himself*, that person shall be cut off from among the assembly, because he has defiled the sanctuary of the LORD. *The water of purification has not been sprinkled on him; he is unclean.*"[3]

---

[1] The Septuagint was an early translation of the Hebrew Bible into Greek. This is the translation that many of the New Testament authors used when quoting from the Old Testament.

[2] This book is sometimes arranged in different order. In the 1611 King James Version Apocrypha, this text will be found in chapter 34:25, 26.

[3] Some still argue that a self-washing was part of the purification, but James Dale answers convincingly:

> But, let us inquire more closely into this "washing." Was it any constituent, at all, in the purification from defilement contracted by "touching a dead body?" We say not: 1. Because the priest who prepared the ashes was required "to wash his clothes and flesh with water and be unclean till even." He had not touched the dead body. 2. He that burned the heifer was required "to wash his clothes and flesh with water and be unclean till the even." He had

The Septuagint was written a couple of hundred years prior to the birth of our Lord, so it is not out of line to assume that the term used for "washing" took on a ceremonial meaning regarding this "washing" of purification. This sprinkling of water mixed with ashes, undoubtedly became known as "baptism." And baptism is just another name for the term "washing," or "purification."

To clearly illustrate this fact, take the Credobaptist to another interesting passage, found early in the Gospel of John, which makes this very point crystal-clear.

> After these things Jesus and His disciples came into the land of Judea, and there He remained with them and **baptized.** Now John also was **baptizing** in Aenon near Salim, because there was much water there. And they came and were **baptized.** For John had not yet been thrown into prison. Then there arose a dispute between some of John's disciples and the Jews about **purification.** And they came to John and said to him, "Rabbi, He who was with you beyond the Jordan, to whom you have testified—behold, He is **baptizing,** and all are coming to Him!" John answered and said, "A man can receive nothing unless it has been given to him from heaven (John 3:22-27).

---

not touched the dead body. 3. He that gathered the ashes was required, "to wash his clothes and be unclean until the even." He had not touched the dead body. 4. He that sprinkled the water of separation was required "to wash his clothes, and he that toucheth the water of separation shall be unclean till even." Neither of these had touched the dead body. When, now, he who had touched a dead body, and had received the appointed means of purification, (the sprinkling of the ashes,) was subsequently required, (in common with all others who had been employed in preparing and dispensing, or accidentally touching this ashes,) "to wash his clothes and flesh," is it not most irrational to consider this as any element in "the purification from a dead body," since it was common to all others, with himself, who had not touched a dead body?

The truth is, that while "the water of separation" had the power "to purify from a dead body," yet in another aspect it had itself the power to make unclean; and therefore, while cleansing from one impurity, its very application made another, and wholly different, cleansing necessary.

That the sole cleansing power "from a dead body" belonged to the heifer ashes, is evident from Hebrews 9:13-14." James W. Dale, Judaic Baptism pg 116.

In this passage, the words "baptism" and "purification" are clearly synonymous.[1] And of course, the word for "purification" is the same word that is used for the "water of purification" in Numbers 19 (in the Septuagint).

This identification cannot be understated to your Credobaptist friend. As pointed out in the last chapter, if you translate the term βαπτίζω as "immerse" throughout the Bible, it sounds silly and makes no sense. But if you translate it by the synonymous term, like "purification," used in John 3, you will see that it all makes perfect sense. (Refer to the section in Chapter 2, entitled "The Word βαπτίζω," for examples.)

Point #2

It was prophesied that someone would come, who would perform this sprinkling of purification on all Israel.

The obligation of this purification law was only done away with at the time of the destruction of Jerusalem in 70 AD. But first, there was a destruction of the temple, which was a foreshadowing of that event. During the captivity of the people of Judah, the prophet Ezekiel prophesied a day of salvation:

---

[1] See Edward Beecher's book *Baptism, with reference to it's Import and Modes* for a thorough exegesis of this passage. Notice also how the New Testament-era historian Josephus speaks about John's baptism. "John, that was called the Baptist...was a good man, and commanded the Jews to exercise virtue, both as to righteousness towards one another, and piety towards God, and so to come to **baptism**; for that the washing [with water] would be acceptable to him, if they made use of it, not in order to the putting away [or the remission] of some sins [only], but for the **purification** of the body; supposing still that the soul was thoroughly **purified** beforehand by righteousness." Antiquities Chapter 8, 5:2.

And I will sanctify My great name, which has been profaned among the nations, which you have profaned in their midst; and the nations shall know that I am the LORD," says the Lord GOD, "when I am hallowed in you before their eyes. For I will take you from among the nations, gather you out of all countries, and bring you into your own land. **Then I will sprinkle clean water on you, and you shall be clean; I will cleanse you from all your filthiness and from all your idols. I will give you a new heart and put a new spirit within you; I will take the heart of stone out of your flesh and give you a heart of flesh. I will put My Spirit within you and cause you to walk in My statutes, and you will keep My judgments and do them.** Then you shall dwell in the land that I gave to your fathers; you shall be My people, and I will be your God" (Ezek. 36:23-28).

The Lord promised to sprinkle *clean* water on them to cleanse them from their filthiness. You see, this is the first time that any Israelite had even heard of being sprinkled with *clean* water for a purification. Why clean water, you ask? Because they only knew of being sprinkled with water that was mixed with blood or ashes.[1] They only knew of dirty water baptisms. Of course, those refer to the sacrifices made to cover sins. But when Christ came, He put those sacrifices away by the most perfect sacrifice that anyone could offer. Thus it's symbolized with pure, clean, "living" water. Now God's people were to be sprinkled with clean water for the very first time.[2] Notice how John the Baptizer fit the bill perfectly. He stressed that his baptism was for "repentance" ("I will take the heart of stone out of your flesh and give you a heart of flesh"), and that he baptized with clean "water" ("I will sprinkle clean water on you"). The people

---

[1] Numbers 19:17; Leviticus 14:6, 51, 52; Hebrews 9:19.

[2] It should be noted that on the day the Church was ratified and 3,000 souls were baptized, they were baptized with *clean* water. When the "church in the wilderness" (Acts 7:38) was ratified at Sinai (Ex. 24:3-8), Moses baptized the people with *bloody* water (Heb. 9:19). This could not have better symbolized the two covenants. And indeed, if this parallel truly exists (and it certainly appears that it does), then we should notice that in the former baptism, all the children— no matter the age—were baptized right along with the rest of the people.

knew that baptism was supposed to have a sacrificial element in it, such as blood or ashes; but not so with John's baptism. His baptism was with clean water, just as Ezekiel had prophesied.

Once the people were back in the land of Israel, there were three more prophets who prophesied prior to the 400-year period that we refer to as the "inter-testamental period"—the time between the last prophet and John the Baptizer. Those three prophets reveal more about the coming "sprinkling" that Ezekiel spoke about.

First, we have Haggai...

> On the twenty-fourth day of the ninth month, in the second year of Darius, the word of the LORD came by Haggai the prophet, saying, "Thus says the LORD of hosts: 'Now, ask the priests concerning the law, saying, "If one carries holy meat in the fold of his garment, and with the edge he touches bread or stew, wine or oil, or any food, will it become holy?"'" Then the priests answered and said, "No." And Haggai said, **"If one who is unclean because of a dead body touches any of these, will it be unclean?"** So the priests answered and said, **"It shall be unclean."** Then Haggai answered and said, **"'So is this people, and so is this nation before Me,'** says the LORD, **'and so is every work of their hands; and what they offer there is unclean'"** (Hag. 2:10-14).

Haggai states quite emphatically that the entire "nation" of Israel is unclean, as having "touched a dead body." It doesn't take a genius to realize that, on the basis of the law in Numbers 19, this statement necessitates that the entire "nation" of Israel needs to be sprinkled with the water of purification, in order to be cleansed from this defilement. John the Baptizer came answering this very call.

Then we have the prophet Zechariah...

> In that day a fountain shall be opened for the house of David and for the inhabitants of Jerusalem, for sin and for uncleanness (Zech. 13:1).

Notice here that Baptists do admit that this passage speaks of baptism, primarily because it doesn't speak of sprinkling. But the word for "uncleanness" is the same word that is used for the water of *purification* in Numbers 19; and that water was also "for sin" (Num. 19:9). So the fountain was not for immersion, but for sprinkling.

Then, of course, we have Malachi...

"Behold, I send My messenger, And he will prepare the way before Me. And the Lord, whom you seek, Will suddenly come to His temple, Even the Messenger of the covenant, In whom you delight. Behold, He is coming," Says the LORD of hosts. "But who can endure the day of His coming? And who can stand when He appears? For He is like a refiner's fire And like launderers' soap. He will sit as a refiner and **a purifier** of silver; **He will purify the** sons of Levi, And purge them as gold and silver, That they may offer to the LORD An offering in righteousness" (Mal. 3:1-3).

Malachi prophesies of a "messenger," who would prepare the way of the Lord. Of course, we recognize that to be John the Baptizer. But then he tells us that the Lord Himself will come after John, and will "purify the sons of Levi" as gold or silver. How are gold and silver purified? By fire, of course. Well, John tells us that Jesus would *baptize* "with the Holy Spirit, *and with fire.*" Interesting, isn't it? The word "purify" here is the same word that is used in Numbers 19 for the water of purification that was sprinkled. There is no mistaking that. The only purifications in the Bible were performed either by water from above, or by *fire*.

Behold, "I will send you Elijah the prophet Before the coming of the great and dreadful day of the LORD. And he will turn The hearts of the fathers to the children, And the hearts of the children to their fathers, Lest I come and strike the earth with a curse" (Mal. 4:5, 6).

Malachi leaves us with the great Elijah prophecy. And the next thing we know, the New Testament opens up, and we are thrust right into the idea of a "prophet"—coming in the likeness of "Elijah"—

and the "Christ," both unified, doing one thing: baptizing with "clean water." This is Christian baptism—a ceremonial purification from death,[1] using clean water that is sprinkled upon the person. Of course, that is not all it is; but it certainly *begins with* a purification— a cleansing.

Point #3

This baptism was a sign of Christ's and our own resurrection.

I find myself in substantial agreement with the great Credobaptist author Alexander Carson, when he states:

> Baptism "is designed to point to our own resurrection, as well as the resurrection of Christ. In Baptism, we profess our faith in the one as past, and in the other as future."[2]

Only, I don't know where Dr. Carson can draw that from Scripture. He can't; he actually made it up, because he has no Biblical data to pull from. Paedobaptists, however, have a Scriptural reason to believe what he stated. This baptism was a cleansing from death. Either you touched a dead body, or you were in a house with a person when they died. You and the entire household wherein the person died, have symbolically contracted death. The picture is clear: sinful men attract death, since death is naturally the wages of sin. When we are around death, we symbolically get it on us. And we need to have the "death" cleaned off of us. That's the picture. Well, what could be a better picture of resurrection than cleaning

---

[1] "Is it not wonderful, too, that death should be washed away by bathing?" Tertullian on Baptism Chpt 2.

[2] Baptism, Its Mode and Subjects. Alexander Carson Pg 144

death off of you?[1] I contract death; I'm dead. I get the death cleansed from me; I'm resurrected. And this picture of resurrection was performed on the third day and on the seventh day. That clearly points toward Christ's resurrection on the third day, and His people's resurrection on the seventh day (the Day of the Lord). And it was by sprinkling—the exact opposite of what Mr. Carson had in mind.

In proof of this contention, notice what Jesus said about how His resurrection was prophesied to take place on the third day.

> Then He said to them, "These are the words which I spoke to you while I was still with you, that all things must be fulfilled **which were written** in the Law of Moses and the Prophets and the Psalms concerning Me." And He opened their understanding, that they might comprehend the Scriptures. Then He said to them, **"Thus it is written,** and thus **it was necessary** for the Christ to suffer and to rise from the dead **the third day"**[2] (Luke 24:44-46).

Obviously, the Bible that Paul had access to was the Old Testament. So where in the Old Testament is it written that Christ's resurrection would take place on the *third day*? Someone may point

---

[1] Notice the difference between us and Jesus. We attract death; He repelled it. When He touched a dead body, it came to life! Instead of attracting death, Jesus exuded life! He couldn't become unclean, because everything He touched became clean!

[2] Also see the following passages:

So the Jews answered and said to Him, "What sign do You show to us, since You do these things?" Jesus answered and said to them, "Destroy this temple, and in three days I will raise it up." Then the Jews said, "It has taken forty-six years to build this temple, and will You raise it up in three days?" But He was speaking of the temple of His body. Therefore, when He had risen from the dead, His disciples remembered that He had said this to them; and **they believed the Scripture** and the word which Jesus had said (John 2:18-22).

For I delivered to you first of all that which I also received: that Christ died for our sins according to the Scriptures, and that He was buried, and that **He rose again the third day according to the Scriptures** (1 Cor. 15:3, 4).

to Jonah, and certainly that counts; but Jesus quite clearly says that it was written "in the Law of Moses" as well as in the Prophets and the Psalms.

You see? This rite represented the resurrection of the Savior on the third day, and the resurrection of His people on the seventh day...*the Day of the Lord.*[1] Every day in Israel, someone was

---

[1] Notice how both Credobaptist and Paedobaptist commentators agree with this interpretation, but they miss one point. All of them rightly point to the seventh-day Sabbath, without recognizing that an all-important event happens at the first day of that eternal Sabbath—*the resurrection of the Church.*

John Gill on Numbers 19:12: "He shall purify himself with it... That is, with the ashes of the water of purification made of them: and this was to be done first on the third day; from the time of his touching the dead body. Aben Ezra intimates, that there is a secret or mystery in this and the following number seven; **it may respect the third day of Christ's resurrection, who, as he shed his blood for the expiation and purification of sinners, so he rose again the third day for the justification of them:** and on the seventh day he shall be clean; **which may denote the perfect state, or sabbath of rest, which remains for the people of God, when all Christ's purified and justified ones shall be clear of all sin, and be the spirits of just men made perfect:** but if he purify not himself the third day, then the seventh day he shall not be clean; whoever is not cleansed from his sins by the blood of Christ, shed for the remission of them, and is not justified from them by him that rose from the dead the third day, will never be cleansed in the world to come, or in the eternal sabbath; but it will then be said, 'Let him that is filthy be filthy still' (Rev. 22:11)."

Matthew Poole on Numbers 19:12: "**On the third day**, to typify Christ's resurrection on that day, by which we are cleansed or sanctified. **On the seventh day** he shall be clean, to teach us that our purification in this life is gradual, and not perfect till we come to that eternal sabbath, which the seventh day respected."

JFB on Numbers 19:12: "He shall purify himself...the third day —The necessity of applying the water **on the third day** is inexplicable on any natural or moral ground; and, therefore, the regulation has been generally supposed to have had a typical reference to the resurrection, on that day, of Christ, by whom His people are sanctified; while the process of ceremonial purification being extended over **seven days**, was intended to show that sanctification is progressive and incomplete till the arrival of the eternal Sabbath. Every one knowingly and presumptuously neglecting to have himself sprinkled with this water was guilty of an offense which was punished by excommunication."

undergoing symbolic resurrection on the third day and on the seventh day. Every day, that is, until the destruction of Jerusalem in 70 AD—which, of course, brings us to our fourth point.

Point #4

This baptism happened until the destruction of Jerusalem in 70 AD.

That's right. This *baptism* happened *every* day of *every* year, multiple times a day, all over Israel and anywhere else where the Jews lived. *It was as ubiquitous as death.* And of course, infants were part of those who needed this baptism as well. After all, they were also in houses when people died. So of course, with the ubiquitous nature of this rite, everyone knew what it was representative of…*new life and resurrection.* And everyone knew how it was performed. They saw it happen over and over again throughout their entire lives. When someone died; everyone who was in that house when the person died, became symbolically dead until they had the death cleansed off of them on the third and the seventh days. And of course, this happened until the destruction of the temple, at which time, the "ashes of a red heifer" became impossible to procure. As Christians, we understand perfectly well *why* this happened. The perfectly pure sacrifice of Christ had come, and bloody water or muddy water was no longer an acceptable symbol of the purification that Christ brings. It must be sparkling *clean.*[1]

---

[1] Look at what the Jews are still saying—even today—about this very baptism. "Full ritual purity of the type needed to enter or serve in the Temple, is not attainable by anyone today, as all are considered to be ritually impure by virtue of exposure to death (via exposure to corpses or to graves and cemeteries, etc.), and that kind of ritual purity can only be obtained when the Jewish people have a Red heifer." http://www.worldheritage.org/article/WHEBN0000555748/Mikveh, 06/22/2018. The poor Jews of today are still looking for someone to sprinkle them with water that is mixed with the ashes of a heifer; and yet Ezekiel told them

In 1 Corinthians 15, the Apostle Paul begins his teaching about the resurrection with a reminder that the third-day resurrection happened "according to the Scriptures" (verse 4). Well, Numbers 19 is exactly where it was written "in the Scriptures" that it would take place on the third day; because the symbol of resurrection, our cleansing from death, takes place on the third day. So we should not be surprised to see that the Apostle Paul references this very baptism at the end of the same section...

> Otherwise, what will they do who are baptized for the dead, if the dead do not rise at all? Why then are they baptized for the dead? (1 Cor. 15:29)

You see? The context is about resurrection; and Paul's point is that if the dead do not rise, why do we still, to this day (when 1 Corinthians was written), see this symbol of resurrection every time someone dies in a Jewish home?[1] Why do they need to seek resurrection, so to speak, from the death which they have contracted? This fits perfectly into the trail of Paul's thought. You have death from Adam, and resurrection from Jesus. Death and anti-death—that is precisely what is pictured in this baptism.

In addition to this, we can also notice some of the surrounding circumstances that emphasize what was happening at this baptism. The red heifer was burned up, along with "cedar wood, and hyssop and scarlet." Everything was the color red. Do I need to point out to anyone that the color red is the color of blood? Blood is *the life*.[2] And it was a heifer. For those of you who may not know, a heifer is a female that has not born offspring yet. Once again, a symbol of *life*.

---

that, after the captivity, God would sprinkle them with "clean water," and they would be cleansed! (See Ezek. 36:25.)

[1] See this argued in detail by Dabney in his Discussions V. 5 Pg 184.

[2] Deuteronomy 12:23.

So everything was meant to symbolize that this was *life* that cleanses us from *death*.

Point #5

This baptism was expected[1]

John the Baptizer believed in *Sola Scriptura,* just like Credobaptists do. Obviously, he would not have deviated from the Levitical Law unless instructed to do so by God. So if the Lord called John to go "baptize," do you think that John would go and do something that no one has ever done before? Or do you think that John would have baptized in the way that the Old Testament baptisms were done? The Old Testament was full of baptisms. The Law prescribed baptisms that affected every person in Israel. These baptisms happened every day in Israel, all the way up to the destruction of the temple in 70 AD. Everybody was familiar with them. Everybody knew how they were performed; not only because the Bible told them how to do it, but also because they saw it on a daily basis.

John knew the Scripture that says, "To the law and to the testimony! If they do not speak according to this word, it is because there is no light in them" (Isa. 8:20). So we must ask our Credobaptist friends to please show us, from John's Bible (the Old Testament, of course), any example of baptism in their understanding of it. But wait—we all agree that one thing must accompany the example: an *administrator.* Washing *yourself* is not the same as having *someone else* wash you. This question needs to be driven home to our Credo brothers. In all the Old Testament (and the New Testament, for that matter), there is not one example of any *person* dunking another *person* in water. None. Nada. Zilch. So how is it that a Jew, a Levite, this son of a priest, would start a brand-new ordinance that the world had never seen before? Of course,

---

[1] Mark 7:3, 4; Luke 11:38; John 1:25.

that didn't happen at all. We know very well that the people had seen it before, because they didn't ask John, "What are you doing?" Instead, they asked, "Who gave you the authority to do it?" Notice the exchange that the Pharisees had with John.

> Now this is the testimony of John, when the Jews sent priests and Levites from Jerusalem to ask him, "Who are you?" He confessed, and did not deny, but confessed, "I am not the Christ." And they asked him, "What then? Are you Elijah?" He said, "I am not." "Are you the Prophet?" And he answered, "No." Then they said to him, "Who are you, that we may give an answer to those who sent us? What do you say about yourself?" He said: "I am 'THE VOICE OF ONE CRYING IN THE WILDERNESS: "MAKE STRAIGHT THE WAY OF THE LORD,"' as the prophet Isaiah said." Now those who were sent were from the Pharisees. And they asked him, saying, **"Why then do you baptize if you are not the Christ, nor Elijah, nor the Prophet?"** (John 1:19-25)

So they knew quite well what it was that John was doing. They apparently knew that the "Christ, Elijah, or the Prophet" would come to do exactly what John was doing. Why? These Pharisees were pretty smart guys, and they were well-versed in the Old Testament Scriptures. So how did they come up with the idea that Christ, Elijah, or the Prophet would be baptizing? You got it—from the texts which I have already shared with you in the second point: this baptism was *prophesied*. They expected someone to come doing exactly what John was doing. If John had been dunking people, they would have had a different reaction. They would have asked *what* he was doing, not *why* he was doing it.

In conclusion, I know of no Credobaptist who would dare to challenge that the law, as laid out in Numbers 19, was not being carried out by the nation of Israel in the time of Christ. That's not to say there *aren't any* who would say this, but I certainly don't *know any.* And there probably will be more people trying to twist their way out of this, the more this argument is promoted. But right now, if we can all agree that it is a proven case that the law in Numbers 19 was still in effect, at least until the destruction of Jerusalem; then we can say with absolute assurance, that **every day** there were ceremonies going on throughout Israel, in which **an administrator** took a bowl full of **water** and a branch of hyssop, and **sprinkled adults and infants**—indeed, entire **households**—in order to cleanse them from the death with which they were defiled. If someone does not wish to call this *baptism,* then tell them to call it what they will. But they will have to admit that it surely looks *very familiar* to what the Paedobaptists are arguing for as baptism.

So if this was a common sight in Israel, all the way up to the destruction of Jerusalem in 70 AD, then the Paedobaptist position is by no means a novelty. If the Credobaptist wants to claim that this was *not* baptism, that's fine; he can do that and present his case. But *at a minimum,* he must acquiesce to *the fact* that infants and adults— yes, entire households—were being sprinkled by an administrator for thousands of years, all the way up to the destruction of the temple in 70 AD. It was ubiquitous as death. There is no way around this painful fact for our Credobaptist brethren. Drive this home, and then move on to the lesser issues that follow.[1]

Seven Days Unclean vs. One Day

As you look at the various cleansing rites in the Bible, you will run into some defilements that made you unclean for that one day alone, and other defilements that made you unclean for seven days. The cleansing ceremonies for these different defilements tell us

---

[1] In contrast, Credobaptists have no idea where to trace the beginnings of im-mersion baptism, other than to John. "We do not know where dipping spiritually renewed people in a pool or stream as a sign of repentance and with reference to sin's cleansing began." Robert Culver, Systematic Theology pg 980

something interesting about what the baptism in Numbers 19 means, and thus, what Christian baptism means.

The defilements that required the defiled person to be unclean for seven days are: the birth of a child (Job 14:4), issues of the flesh, death in the house, touching a dead body, and leprosy. The defilements that required a single day of uncleanness are too many to list here, but they included sexual relations and other things related to discharges and such.[1] You can see that the more impressive defilements required *another person* to cleanse the defiled person. This is because they represent our inward corruption, and only God can cleanse that away. Thus, we have an administrator to do the cleansing, in order to represent God cleansing the heart. The same-day cleansings were representative of cleansing yourself. These represent our own efforts toward sanctification. Remember when Jesus said, "He who is bathed needs only to wash his feet, but is completely clean." The person was cleansed by Jesus, but he had to continually wash the filth of walking through this wicked world off of his person. He could do this himself. And so the same-day cleansings were essentially nothing more than taking a shower and doing the laundry. Contrary to this, the more serious defilements not only needed to be done by another person, but it also was not sufficient for the defiled person to merely take a shower and do the laundry; they needed to be baptized as well. They needed this water of purification.

This water of purification was used with any administered cleansing, not just for when you touched something dead. It was also used for the baptism of the Levites...

Take the Levites from among the children of Israel and **cleanse them ceremonially**. Thus you shall do to them to cleanse them: **Sprinkle water of purification on them**, and let them shave all their body, and let them wash their clothes, and so make themselves clean (Num. 8:6, 7).

---

[1] See the section in Chapter 6 on "The Self Washings."

It was also used on the spoils of war...

"And as for you, remain outside the camp seven days; whoever has killed any person, and whoever has touched any slain, purify yourselves and your captives on the third day and on the seventh day. **Purify every garment, everything made of leather, everything woven of goats' hair, and everything made of wood."** Then Eleazar the priest said to the men of war who had gone to the battle, "This is the ordinance of the law which the LORD commanded Moses: 'Only the gold, the silver, the bronze, the iron, the tin, and the lead, everything that can endure fire, you shall put through the fire, and it shall be clean; and **it shall be purified with the water of purification.** But all that cannot endure fire you shall put through water. And you shall wash your clothes on the seventh day and be clean, and afterward you may come into the camp'" (Num. 31:19-24).

Even when David felt the overwhelming shame of guilt, he asked God to "wash" him. This was not a self-washing; it was administered by God, and it was by sprinkling.

Have mercy upon me, O God, According to Your lovingkindness; According to the multitude of Your tender mercies, Blot out my transgressions. **Wash me thoroughly from my iniquity, And cleanse me from my sin.** For I acknowledge my transgressions, And my sin is always before me. Against You, You only, have I sinned, And done this evil in Your sight—That You may be found just when You speak, And blameless when You judge. Behold, I was brought forth in iniquity, And in sin my mother conceived me. Behold, You desire truth in the inward parts, And in the hidden part You will make me to know wisdom. **Purge me with hyssop, and I shall be clean; Wash me,** and I shall be whiter than snow (Ps. 51:1-7).

This is why we know that baptism in the New Testament was by effusion. It was an *administered* cleansing, and the only administered cleansing in the Bible is by effusion.

Living Water

I would like to dwell for just a moment on water. It was a pretty important commodity in Israel, just like it is everywhere. It's necessary for life. Thus, it's a fitting symbol for life, cleansing, and the life given by the life-giver. And our Lord uses water to illustrate that very thing. He talks about the "living water"; that is, the Holy Spirit.

> Jesus answered and said to her, "If you knew the gift of God, and who it is who says to you, 'Give Me a drink,' you would have asked Him, and **He would have given you living water"** (John 4:10).

> Jesus answered and said to her, "Whoever drinks of this water will thirst again, but whoever drinks of the water that I shall give him will never thirst. **But the water that I shall give him will become in him a fountain of water springing up into everlasting life"** (John 4:13, 14).

> On the last day, that great day of the feast, Jesus stood and cried out, saying, "If anyone thirsts, let him come to Me and drink. He who believes in Me, as the Scripture has said, out of his heart will flow **rivers of living water."** But **this He spoke concerning the Spirit,** whom those believing in Him would receive; for the Holy Spirit was not yet given, because Jesus was not yet glorified (John 7:37-39).

Rain is also representative of God's blessings. God Himself is said to come to us like the rain...

> **He shall come down like rain upon the grass before mowing, Like showers that water the earth** (Ps. 72:6).

> Let us know, Let us pursue the knowledge of the LORD. His going forth is established as the morning; **He will come to us like the rain, Like the latter and former rain to the earth** (Hos. 6:3).

Rain is a symbol; for it is life from above, proceeding from heaven.

> For the land which you go to possess is not like the land of Egypt from which you have come, where you sowed your seed and watered it by foot, as a vegetable garden; but the land which you cross over to possess is a land of hills and valleys, **which drinks water from the rain of heaven,** a land for which the LORD your God cares; the eyes of the LORD your God are always on it, from the beginning of the year to the very end of the year (Deut. 11:10-12).

> For **the earth which drinks in the rain that often comes upon it,** and bears herbs useful for those by whom it is cultivated, receives blessing from God; but if it bears thorns and briers, it is rejected and near to being cursed, whose end is to be burned (Heb. 6:7, 8).

In Scripture, rain is always viewed as a blessing.

> Be glad then, you children of Zion, And rejoice in the LORD your God; For **He has given you the former rain faithfully**, And He **will cause the rain to come down for you**—The former rain, And the latter rain in the first month[1] (Joel 2:23).

> If you walk in My statutes and keep My commandments, and perform them, then **I will give you rain in its season,** the land shall yield its produce, and the trees of the field shall yield their fruit[2] (Lev. 26:3).

Likewise, the absence of rain is viewed as a curse.

---

[1] Just a couple of verses later, in parallel to this promised latter-day rain, the Lord says, "And it shall come to pass afterward That I will pour out My Spirit on all flesh; Your sons and your daughters shall prophesy, Your old men shall dream dreams, Your young men shall see visions" (Joel 2:28).

[2] Also see Leviticus 26:4; Deuteronomy 11:14; 28:12; Proverbs 16:15; Zechariah 10:1.

Son of man, say to her: "You are a land that is not cleansed **or rained on** in the day of indignation" (Ezek. 22:24).

Therefore **the showers have been withheld, And there has been no latter rain.** You have had a harlot's forehead; You refuse to be ashamed[1] (Jer. 3:3).

This *water from above* is a picture of God's blessing of the Holy Spirit. Note well the mode of both blessings being distributed.

For **I will pour water on him who is thirsty,** And floods on the dry ground; **I will pour My Spirit on your descendants,** And My blessing on your offspring (Isa. 44:3).

Water symbolizes the Holy Spirit, proceeding from the throne of God and the Lamb.

And in that day it shall be—**That living waters shall flow from Jerusalem,** Half of them toward the eastern sea And half of them toward the western sea; In both summer and winter it shall occur (Zech. 14:8).

And he showed me **a pure river of water of life,** clear as crystal, **proceeding from the throne of God and of the Lamb** (Rev. 22:1).

There is a river whose streams shall make glad the city of God, The holy place of the tabernacle of the Most High (Ps. 46:4).

But when the Helper comes, whom I shall send to you from the Father, **the Spirit of truth who proceeds from the Father,** He will testify of Me (John 15:26).

---

[1] Also see Haggai 1:11; Amos 4:7; Isaiah 5:6; Deuteronomy 28:23; Leviticus 26:19.

These rivers consist of pure water; there is "no more sea," containing salty, bitter water.

> Now I saw a new heaven and a new earth, for the first heaven and the first earth had passed away. Also **there was no more sea** (Rev. 21:1).

With the tremendous testimony of Scripture telling us that water is representative of the Holy Spirit and the life He brings, do you really think that it's appropriate to imagine that the Apostle Paul would then turn this beautiful symbol of life and the Holy Spirit into a putrid, stinking grave? Really? I guess we could agree that from a certain perspective, Credobaptists may have a point. Once, God did use water as a grave, for nearly the entire population of humanity. But I don't believe that our Credobaptist brethren really want to use baptism as a picture of judgment.[1]

Tour de Acts

I'm sure you've heard of the Romans Road, a method of sharing the Gospel with people, using several passages found in the book of Romans. Well, I have a similar exercise that may help your Credobaptist brethren understand that the New Testament actually

---

[1] Is the water of baptism a sign of God's judgment? Wayne Grudem argues that it is. He says that your baptism is a sign that you have safely gone through the waters of judgment. He then points to 1 Peter 3:21, and says that this is where the correspondence comes from. (Systematic Theology pg 968 note 7.) Mr. Grudem has certainly given us something to chew on, hasn't he? But then we must spit it out. Those who were sprinkled were the ones who escaped the judgment of God through Christ, the true Ark. That is how the Bible shows escape from the flood of judgment, not at all by being immersed and withdrawn. Those who were immersed did not escape judgment. Do you ever remember someone being afraid of rain in the Bible? Of course not. But how many times were they afraid of drowning in the sea? Water from above—good; going under the water—bad.

does explicitly state the mode of baptism. Have your friend open his Bible to the book of Acts, and do a *tour de acts*.

First, show your friend that it was Jesus Himself Who promised a "baptism."

> And being assembled together with them, He commanded them not to depart from Jerusalem, but to wait for the Promise of the Father, "which," He said, "you have heard from Me; for **John truly baptized with water, but you shall be baptized with the Holy Spirit** not many days from now" (Acts 1:4, 5).

Next, show them what happened when this took place on the day of Pentecost:

> When the Day of Pentecost had fully come, they were all with one accord in one place. And suddenly there came a sound from heaven, as of a rushing mighty wind, and it filled the whole house where they were sitting...But Peter, standing up with the eleven, raised his voice and said to them, "Men of Judea and all who dwell in Jerusalem, let this be known to you, and heed my words. For these are not drunk, as you suppose, since it is only the third hour of the day. But **this is what was spoken by the prophet Joel**: 'AND IT SHALL COME TO PASS IN THE LAST DAYS, SAYS GOD, THAT I WILL **POUR OUT OF MY SPIRIT** ON ALL FLESH; YOUR SONS AND YOUR DAUGHTERS SHALL PROPHESY, YOUR YOUNG MEN SHALL SEE VISIONS, YOUR OLD MEN SHALL DREAM DREAMS. AND ON MY MENSERVANTS AND ON MY MAIDSERVANTS I WILL **POUR OUT MY SPIRIT** IN THOSE DAYS; AND THEY SHALL PROPHESY'" (Acts 2:1, 2, 14-18).

Then show them what happened when the Gentiles experienced this baptism as well:

> While Peter was still speaking these words, the **Holy Spirit fell upon** all those who heard the word. And those of the circumcision

who believed were astonished, as many as came with Peter, because the gift of **the Holy Spirit had been poured out** on the Gentiles also. For they heard them speak with tongues and magnify God. Then Peter answered, "Can anyone forbid water, that these should not be **baptized** who have received the Holy Spirit just as we have?" And he commanded them to be **baptized** in the name of the Lord. Then they asked him to stay a few days (Acts 10:44-48).

And finally, show them how Peter described this very event:

And as I began to speak, the Holy Spirit **fell upon** them, as upon us at the beginning. **Then I remembered** the word of the Lord, how He said, '**John indeed baptized with water**, but **you shall be baptized with the Holy Spirit**' (Acts 11:15, 16).

All right, so the tour started with Jesus saying, "You shall be baptized with the Holy Spirit"; and it ended with Peter remembering Jesus saying, "You shall be baptized with the Holy Spirit." Now, look through the texts and tell me if it's not explicitly stated, numerous times, how that baptism took place. Point out to your brethren that it was this "pouring out" and falling "upon," that triggered Peter's memory to recall how Jesus said they would be baptized. It explicitly says that the Holy Spirit "fell upon them" and "us," and it was that event which caused Peter to remember Jesus saying that they would "be baptized with the Holy Spirit." It doesn't get much easier than this.

Chapter 4

The Biblical Status of our Children

It is the contention of some Baptists that the children of believers are not members of the Church until they reach an arbitrary "age of accountability," and consciously choose to enter into the Church. Until such a time, they say, they are to be considered no different from the children of heathen homes. In this chapter, it is my purpose to show you that the children of believers are to be considered members of the Church of Jesus Christ, and not merely as heathens.

Are they God's people?

For you are **a holy people** to the Lord your God; the Lord your **God has chosen you to be a people for Himself, a special treasure** above all the peoples on the face of the earth (Deut. 7:6).

Throughout both Testaments, the people of God are called many different things: Israel, the children of Israel, Zion, Jacob, the Church, etc. In the Old Testament, God's people were confined to one particular physical nation. Now, however, God's people are from every physical nation on earth, and have no one particular geographical location. There are many other discontinuities between the Testaments (such as the absence of a physical temple, sacrifices, etc.), but there is much continuity as well. Notice how 1 Peter 2:9 compares to the verse from Deuteronomy, quoted above.

> But you are **a chosen generation,** a royal priesthood, **a holy nation, His own special people,** that you may proclaim the praises of Him who called you out of darkness into His marvelous light (1 Pet. 2:9).

Do you see how Peter echoes the thought of Deuteronomy 7:6? The Church is called the "people" of God, just as Israel was called the "people" of God. But what does Peter mean by using the terms "people" and "nation"? Does Peter mean something *entirely different* from what Moses meant as far as the use of those terms? You see, in the Old Testament, the "people of God" included all the children of all believers. Notice:

> Blow the trumpet in Zion, consecrate a fast, call a sacred assembly; gather **the people,** sanctify the congregation, assemble the elders, gather the children **and nursing babes;** let the bridegroom go out from his chamber, and the bride from her dressing room. Let the priests, who minister to the Lord, weep between the porch and the altar; let them say, "Spare **Your people,** O Lord, and do not give Your heritage to reproach" (Joel 2:15-17).

Here in Joel 2, you see that the "people" of the Lord included "nursing babes". Where is the evidence that this is no longer the case in the New Testament? Do you know how many times I have heard Baptists quote Old Testament texts that speak of God's *people* as if it applies directly to the Church, and yet they deny God's very definition of the term *people?* For example...

We are His people and the sheep of His pasture (Ps. 100:3).

The people that the Psalmist is speaking of, includes infants. Could anybody challenge that? Go ahead and ask your Baptist brother to see how many Old Testament passages he knows by heart which speak of God's people. Then ask if he's ever used the same definition of the word *people* as the definition that God uses? What about...

> For you are the temple of the living God. As God has said: "I WILL DWELL IN THEM AND WALK AMONG THEM. I WILL BE THEIR GOD, AND THEY SHALL BE MY PEOPLE" (2 Cor. 6:16).

Here, the Apostle Paul is clearly comparing the New Testament Church to the Old Testament Church. *"You,"* he says, "are the temple of the living God." That means, *"you,"* the Church of Jesus Christ. And he proves his point by quoting from the following verses:

> I will dwell among the children of Israel and will be their God (Ex. 29:45).

> I will walk among you and be your God, and you shall be **My people** (Lev. 26:12).

> My tabernacle also shall be with **them**; indeed I will be **their** God, and **they** shall be **My people** (Ezek. 37:27).

So once again, we ask our Credobaptist brethren to show us any indication from the Bible, that when the Apostle actually quotes from the Old Testament and applies it to the New Testament Church, he is defining the words *differently* from the way in which they were defined in the Old Testament. "I WILL DWELL IN **THEM** AND WALK AMONG **THEM**. I WILL BE **THEIR** GOD, AND **THEY** SHALL BE **MY PEOPLE**." All of those terms included the children in the Old Testament Church; where is the indication that these terms do not include the children now?

How can a Baptist consistently apply these texts to the Church, when their very definition of the word *church* excludes children!? Only someone of the Paedobaptist persuasion can *consistently* apply those texts of Scripture to the Church today, because they are using the same definition of the term "people" as the one that God assigned to it: the believers *and* their children.

So now the Baptist must prove that the definition of the terms *people* and *nation* have somehow changed, from the way in which the prophets used them to the way in which the Apostles used them.

Do you think that Peter the Jew (or any of the Apostles, for that matter) meant anything other than what was taught in the Old Testament by the term *people*? If so, why do they never discuss it? When Peter used the phrase "holy nation," did he intend for us to use a definition of the word *nation* that had never before been used? Have you ever heard of a *nation* that did not include children? The Apostles had the clear teachings of the Old Testament, which include infants of believers in the "people of God." If they meant something else, then they should tell us somewhere that it is not that way anymore, and that they meant something radically different than what the Old Testament meant. It is the Paedobaptists contention that when Peter and the rest of the Apostles spoke of the people of God, they meant the exact same thing that the Old Testament taught them that it meant: believers *and* their children. If your Baptist brother finds it to be otherwise, then ask him to present his Biblical proof.

Case in point: I have a wonderful Baptist friend who quotes 2 Chronicles 7:14 on his voice mail message: "If My people who are called by My name will humble themselves, and pray and seek My face, and turn from their wicked ways, then I will hear from heaven, and will forgive their sin and heal their land." My friend obviously means to say that this text applies to "us Christians," and that we are the "people" that this passage is referring to. But the "people" that this passage is referring to, includes the *children*. If the Bible does not specifically change the meaning of a term, then you can be absolutely certain that it is still defined in the same way when the New Testament authors use it. When the New Testament authors use the terms "people," "nation," and "generation," you can rest assured that they intended to include the children; because *their* Bible (the Old Testament) included the children in those terms.

LOVED BY GOD BECAUSE OF ME?

All Paedobaptist apologists should have the following verse committed to memory.

> And because He loved your fathers, therefore He chose their descendants after them (Deut. 4:37).

Wow, I can think of no greater statement in Scripture to show the clear relationship that our children have with God. If we are beloved of God, *then so... are... our... children*. This should be no surprise. Of course, we are not interfering with God's sovereignty by saying that they are beloved by God. It is a sad fact that many of the Church's children have apostatized and gone to an eternal punishment. And yet they were still placed in this covenant relationship with God. They were placed in *His Church*.

This is nothing to be afraid of. Rather, it's to be celebrated. And as you celebrate it, your Credobaptist friends will see you celebrate it; and they will wonder why they don't celebrate it, even though they feel the same way about their children. They know that God loves their children because He loves them. *They know it*. You just need to show them that it's a good thing to *admit*.

Make sure that you yourself get the strength of this passage, so that you can pass on the beauty of it to your Credobaptist brethren. It says that God "chose their descendants after them" BECAUSE "He loved your fathers." Don't miss the correlation. He has given them a special privilege and status BECAUSE of the relationship which He had with their fathers.

Notice that the Lord doesn't have any problem saying that He loved "His people." We shouldn't, either. Even the famous Credobaptist commentator John Gill had no problem correctly expounding this verse in his commentary.

> Therefore he chose their seed after them; not to eternal life and salvation, but to the enjoyment of **external blessings and**

privileges, to be **called by his name**, and to **set up his name and worship among them**, and **to be a special people to him** above all people on the earth, as to **outward favors, both civil and ecclesiastical.**

I fully concur with this famous Credobaptist's comment. This is precisely the doctrine of the Paedobaptist Church on the status of our children. We do not believe that our children, by default, have a one-way ticket to heaven. We believe that God has placed his lovingkindness upon them, *because* He loves us. According to John Gill, the children of this people have the following blessings, due to the love which God had toward their fathers:

1. They have "external blessings and privileges."
2. They are "called by his name."
3. God has "set up his name and worship among them."
4. They are His own "special people."
5. This peoplehood includes "outward favors, both civil and ecclesiastical."

I don't know that I could more fully agree with his synopsis of this people's blessings. Many of our Credobaptist brethren would like to say that these blessings were only upon the nation of Israel as a physical nation. I don't really care what they say, because the text tells us exactly *why* they had these blessings. It's the *why* that is important here. It says, *"because* He loved your fathers." And that reason has never been rescinded. God does not feel differently about *your* children now, than He did with the children of the Israelites. The Lord *chooses* the "descendants" of those whom He loves.[1] This is equally true with *your* children. Observe:

---

[1] I understand that this can be construed by some to mean that they are eternally elect unto salvation. I do not believe that. That is in the hidden council of our God and I do not presume to know my children are written in the lambs book of life. I only know that he has placed them into a special relationship with himself he refers to as "his people" and "chosen". But that should not be confused with eternal election unto salvation.

1. They have "external blessings and privileges," such as being a family that worships Christ, and having the Word of God read to them daily. (You do read it with them daily, don't you?)
2. They are "called by his name," that of a "Christian."
3. God has "set up his name and worship among them," by setting them solidly in the Church of Jesus Christ, where His Word is preached and His sacraments administered.
4. They are His own "special people," according to 1 Peter 2:9, 10.
5. This peoplehood includes "outward favors, both civil and ecclesiastical." Examples of these favors would include peaceful nations because their parents pay their taxes and abide by the laws, and also having all of the outward means of grace in the Church.

What more does the Paedobaptist want? This quote from John Gill's Bible commentary is a wonderful statement on the status of our covenant children; and if all of our Credobaptist brethren would adopt this particular view of one of *their* "fathers," then they would only be a hair's breadth away from being a Paedobaptist.

ARE THEY "HOLY, HOLY, HOLY"?

The first words spoken by my fourth child were, "Holy, holy, holy." She was singing the song that our family sang in our family worship time. Out of the lips of my babe came forth praise to the thrice-holy God, and she still loves to sing God's praises. The first word that my fifth child spoke was a hearty "Amen!" I have no trouble attributing that to the Spirit of God dwelling within my children. After all, the Apostle Paul told me that they are "holy."

> For the unbelieving husband is sanctified by the wife, and the unbelieving wife is sanctified by the husband; otherwise your **children** would be unclean, but now they are **holy** (1 Cor. 7:14).

Now, we must ask our Baptist brethren to forget all the myriad of explanations that they have heard on this verse. It doesn't really matter what "holy" means here. What matters is that *our* children are "holy" to the Lord, *whatever* it means. That means that God has set our children apart into some special relationship with Himself, by putting them into a family where they will be raised to know Him. I like to ask my Baptist brethren if they really believe that it is God Who has given them their children? Or if they think that they were born into their home by chance? They know as well as we do, that our God has placed these children in our homes by His own sovereign power. God could have placed them in a pagan home somewhere in San Francisco, so that they could learn that it is right to have two dads or something. But He didn't. He graciously placed them in a home where He knew that they would be taught to live for Him! It was no accident! He has chosen our children for Himself, and separated them from among the world by putting them in our care. Doesn't that tell us that God thinks differently about *our* children than He does about our heathen neighbor's children? I know, people want to say, "God loves all the little children of the world". But God calls our children "holy," and He calls your neighbors' children "unclean." Knowing this fact places a huge burden upon the fathers to be extra-diligent when it comes to raising our children. Remember that God has *not* given us those children *so that they will have better chances to become Christians*; He has given us those children because He has already claimed them *for Himself,* and expects us to raise them *as holy persons!* If your children apostatize and leave Christ behind, then you have either failed in your commission, and not trained them in the way they should go; or else they are the worst of mankind, and have spurned the God whom they have been raised to know. Either way, they will be considered *covenant-breakers.* So how is it, then, you ask, that we are to raise them?

Hear, O Israel: The Lord our God, the Lord is one! You shall love the Lord your God with all your Heart, with all your soul, and with all your strength. And these words which I command you today shall be in your heart. **You shall teach them diligently to your children, and shall talk of them when you sit in your house, when you walk by the way, when you lie down, and when you rise up.** You shall bind them as a sign on your hand, and they shall be as frontlets between your eyes. You shall write them on the doorposts of your house and on your gates (Deut. 6:4-9).

For all of those who question whether or not they have raised up their children "in the training and admonition of the Lord" sufficiently enough to know that they will "not depart from it," we have this exhortation from Moses. The key, Moses says, is diligence—not just taking your children to Church on Sunday, but having your entire lives consumed with training your children to know God and His Word.

Notice the Lord's conversation with Abraham:

For I have known him, in order that he may command his children and his household after him, that they keep the way of the Lord, to do righteousness and justice (Gen.18:19).

You see, God had a specific purpose for Abraham's children, so He placed them in Abraham's lineage. This shows us God's heart towards *our* children. He desires us to raise them to keep the way of the Lord. That is not only what is best for your children, but it is also what the Lord desires.

THE COVENANT

When God covenanted with His people, He clearly included *all* of His people, including the children of those who were His. Ask your Baptist brother if he thinks that God has changed His mind and now says, "You know, I don't think this 'covenanting with the children' thing is working very well; maybe I should try something else…"? Should we even entertain the idea that God's way of doing things could have been wrong, and that He has learned lessons from His mistakes?

> All of you stand today before the Lord your God: your leaders and your tribes and your elders and your officers, all the men of Israel, **your little ones** and your wives—also the stranger who is in your camp, from the one who cuts your wood to the one who draws your water—that you may enter into covenant with the Lord your God, and into His oath, which the Lord your God makes with you today (Deut. 29:10-12).

The "covenant" was made with all of Israel—all the people of the Lord. This included "little ones." Baptists sometimes object that the servants and strangers were also included in the Old Testament covenants; and because we would not include them today, we should not apply those covenants to the New Covenant believers. I absolutely agree that strangers and servants were indeed included in the Old Testament covenants, but I object to saying that we do not include them today. As a matter of fact, the New Testament covenant includes them just as well as the Old. Any "strangers" that I might have staying in my house fall under my headship, and would therefore be included in the covenant. I don't have a problem with that, because I am consistent in my Biblical belief. Baptists object by saying, "But how can these heathen strangers be included in Christ's covenant?" To which I reply, "They aren't." You see, even in the Old Testament, the *heathen* were not in covenant with God; the strangers and servants that the Scripture speaks about were not heathens. *They were believers. Anyone*—whether native-born or strangers—*anyone* who rejected Jehovah was cast out of the land, or "cut off."

> You shall have one law for him who sins unintentionally, for him who is native-born among the children of Israel and for the stranger who dwells among them. 'But the person who does anything presumptuously, **whether he is native-born or a stranger**, that

one brings reproach on the LORD, and **he shall be cut off from among his people.** Because he has despised the word of the LORD, and has broken His commandment, that person shall be completely cut off; his guilt shall be upon him'" (Num. 15:29-31).

Now **the man who acts presumptuously** and **will not heed the priest** who stands to minister there before the LORD your God, or the judge, **that man shall die.** So you shall put away the evil from Israel (Deut. 17:12).

If your brother, the son of your mother, **your son or your daughter,** the wife of your bosom, **or your friend who is as your own soul,** secretly entices you, saying, "Let us go and serve other gods," which you have not known, neither you nor your fathers, of the gods of the people which are all around you, near to you or far off from you, from one end of the earth to the other end of the earth, you shall not consent to him or listen to him, nor shall your eye pity him, nor shall you spare him or conceal him; but **you shall surely kill him;** your hand shall be first against him to put him to death, and afterward the hand of all the people. And you shall stone him with stones until he dies, because he sought to entice you away from the LORD your God, who brought you out of the land of Egypt, from the house of bondage. So all Israel shall hear and fear, and not again do such wickedness as this among you (Deut. 13:6-15).

That rule applied to **strangers, servants, wives,** and **children.** Thus, if a stranger or servant dwells with me and is a believer, I will consider it a privilege to baptize him if he has not been already. If that stranger or servant dwells with me and proves himself a heathen, I will consider it a duty to expel him from the covenant promises and my house. And how do we determine whether they are heathen or not? By obedience, of course. (More on this later.)

The secret things belong to the Lord our God, but those things which are revealed belong to us and to our children forever, that we may do all the words of this law (Deut. 29:29).

The "things which are revealed"? God's revelation belongs to Christians, does it not? Joshua knew that because it belonged to *him,* it belonged to his children as well. How many of our Baptist brethren feel that way? And so we can ask our Baptist Brethren if God's blessings belong to *their* children simply because they belong to them? *Is the United States of America truly more gracious than our Triune God?* After all, the USA (and all other nations, for that matter) grants our children citizenship, simply on the basis that *they belong to us.* Is our God really less gracious? Remember that if a child of ours grows up and betrays his nation, he will be stripped of his citizenship. It's the same way with God's covenant. Our children are considered complete citizens, fully worthy of baptism, until they betray the covenant; at which point, they either repent or are cut off from the citizenship of the Kingdom of God.

Are they "the Saints"?

We have all undoubtedly read the New Testament Epistles so many times, that we can almost quote the opening lines in just about all of them. The Pauline Epistles all say something like, "Grace to you and peace"; and they all start with whom the letter is written *by,* and then they tell us whom it's written *to.* And when it tells us whom it is written to, it always addresses the Epistle to a particular person or an entire group. For instance, the Epistle to the Ephesian church is addressed like this: "To the saints who are in Ephesus, and faithful in Christ Jesus." Do we think that Paul, after addressing himself to the "saints," would then speak directly to someone whom he knew was *not* a saint? It's entirely proper to speak *to* the saints *about* the heathen; Paul does this all the time. But Paul maintains proper letter-writing etiquette, and never speaks directly to anyone other than the one to whom the epistle was written. If I wrote to you, "Dear (enter your name)," you might not think it was weird for me to ask you to tell your sister hello. But what if you were reading this letter that I wrote to you, and I suddenly started speaking directly to your sister?

Wouldn't that be kind of weird? Well, Baptists must believe that Paul did just that. They must believe that in a letter written to "the saints," Paul spoke directly to those who do not belong to the Church.

To prove this point, notice that the Apostle Paul called our children "saints" and "faithful brethren in Christ" when he spoke directly to them in a letter addressed to "saints" and "faithful brethren." Paul addressed his letter to the Ephesians to the "saints who are in Ephesus, and faithful in Christ Jesus." Then, in this same epistle, Paul says, "Children, obey your parents in the Lord, for this is right." Press that point home to your Baptist Brother—he actually called our children "saints" and "faithful in Christ Jesus."

Again, Paul addressed the "saints and faithful brethren in Christ" when he wrote his epistle to the Colossians. There the Apostle is bold enough to address our children once again. "Children, obey your parents in all things, for this is well pleasing to the Lord." Hmm, that means that Paul called our children "faithful brethren in Christ." If children were not considered "saints," then Paul should have said something like this: "You fathers, tell your children that I said they should obey their parents." He didn't need to do that, because he considered children to be part of the church to whom his Epistle was addressed.

"But Paul, my children aren't Christians. Why should they be concerned about pleasing the Lord?" Do you think it's strange that someone would say that? Some Baptist friends of mine gave my family a book that made that same case. The little girl in the book, who was being instructed to be modest, said, "But why do I have to do that? I haven't been converted; I'm not a Christian yet!" To which the adult (whom the child was addressing) replied, that although she was not a Christian yet, she should dress modestly anyway, just in case she does become a Christian someday. What absurd reasoning! But it is a good example of the confusion that Baptist theology brings with it.

Are they to be forbidden? "βρέφος"

I believe Luke 18:15-17 clinches the argument that Christ considers infants to be in the Church. Here it is:

> Then they also brought infants to Him that He might touch them; but when the disciples saw it, they rebuked them. But Jesus called them to Him and said, "Let the little children come to me, and do not forbid them; for of such is the kingdom of God. Assuredly, I say to you, whoever does not receive the kingdom of God as a little child will by no means enter it.

This is a famous passage in the infant baptism debate. The Paedobaptists say, "You see, they are in the kingdom of God." And the Credobaptists answer, "This passage is only showing us that we need to have the faith of a little child to get into heaven." Back and forth it goes, on and on and on, *ad nauseum*.

I, however, take a different approach to this text. I am first going to attack the Baptist position, which claims that this passage teaches that we "need to have the faith of a little child to get into heaven." We have all heard this interpretation; and we have all pictured in our minds a little 3-year-old child, jumping into his father's hands with complete trust that he will be caught by his father. What a sweet picture, and we say, "We need to have the same trust in our heavenly Father." Amen! What faith! But is that what Christ was teaching us?

Most people take it for granted that that is exactly what Jesus was saying, because that is what they have been taught. But they have failed to take into account the very *words* of Jesus here. The disciples were bringing **infants** to Christ! Not just 3-year-olds…but also newborns! How could Jesus be teaching a "child-like faith," when He was referring to *infants*? At this point, the Credobaptist has two routes to take in order to get around this glaring fact. Let's examine both.

First, they could deny that there were actual *newborns* in the crowd. Let's see if that is an option. The Greek word "βρέφος" is used only eight times in the Bible. Let's examine them.

Luke 1:41, 44: "the babe in her womb" (John the Baptizer, pre-born)
Luke 2:12, 16: "a babe wrapped in swaddling clothes" (our Lord, newborn)
Acts 7:19: "expose their babies" (the newborn male Hebrew children)
1 Peter 2:2: "as newborn babes" (desire the milk)
2 Tim 3:15: "from childhood you have known the Holy Scriptures" (from infancy, showing the covenantal care that Timothy had)

The eighth passage in which the word is used, is right here in Luke 18:15. So infants were, *beyond a doubt,* some of those children whom Jesus was talking about. Objection Number 1 is overruled.

The second objection that a Baptist could raise, is to say that infants do indeed have a "child-like faith"; thus their interpretation stands. That seems reasonable to me. As a matter of fact, I would agree with the assertion that infants have a "child-like faith." But of course, if Baptists were to admit that same assertion, they would be robbing themselves of their main argument *against* baptizing infants. In other words, if infants do indeed have a "child-like faith," then they would not be able to use "lack of faith" as an argument against baptizing them. Objection Number 2 is overruled.

So what was Jesus teaching, if it wasn't a "child-like faith"? The answer is easy; look at what He actually *said.*

Whoever does not *receive* the kingdom of God as a little child will by no means enter it.

You see, an infant can do nothing to claim a right to enter into the kingdom; he must *receive* it as a gift from Christ's own hand. It's all because of the grace of God. The child has done nothing to deserve entrance into the kingdom, and he does not even try to earn his way; he simply receives that which has been given to him, with joy. We all must receive the kingdom in the same way, without any attempt to earn it. It's given to us; and we rejoice in it, without having any involvement in how we got there. We just accept and love the fact that we are there...*like a little child!*

Such and such: "τοιοῦτος"

In the same passage we've been discussing (Luke 18:15-17), we must make our Credobaptist brethren consider the word "such." When Jesus says, "For of *such* is the kingdom of God," does the word "such" convey the meaning that Baptists want to claim that it does? They give it the meaning of "*like* these children," in such a manner that the children *themselves* are not included. In other words, you need to have "characteristics of these children." But notice, once again, how the Bible uses the term differently than what they assert. Look at some other places where it is used.

When the Jews tested Jesus about the woman caught in adultery, they said to Him,

> Now Moses, in the law, commanded us that **such** should be stoned. But what do You say? (John 8:5)

Did they mean that only those *like* this woman were to be stoned, or both this woman *and* all like her?

> And they listened to him until this word, and then they raised their voices and said, "Away with **such** a fellow from the earth, for he is not fit to live!" (Acts 22:22)

In this case, if the word "such" means what Baptists say it means in Luke 18, then Paul is perfectly safe; because then it would only mean that other people *like* Paul were in danger, but not Paul *himself*. But we all know that Paul's life *was* in danger, because they meant "Paul *and* all like him" when they said "such."

I urge you, brethren—you know the household of Stephanas, that it is the firstfruits of Achaia, and that they have devoted themselves to the ministry of the saints—that you also submit to **such,** they refreshed my spirit and yours. Therefore acknowledge **such** men (1 Cor. 16:15, 16, 18).

Did Paul mean that we are to submit and acknowledge those *like* Stephanas, or Stephanas himself *and* all like him? You know very well that we could paraphrase Paul by saying, "I urge you to submit to and acknowledge Stephanas *and* all who are like him."

So now, let's take another look at the verse at hand.

Let the little children come to me, and do not forbid them; for of **such** is the kingdom of God.

Christ is saying, "These little children *and* all like them (covenant children) are in the kingdom of God." The word "such" is the same Greek word that is used in all of the examples above. Here is yet another example of where we must let the Word of God declare for us how a term is to be interpreted, and how we are to understand a passage. Jesus considered these little children—yes, even the infants—to be in the Kingdom of God—the Church.

Believe it or not, even Menno Simons, the great leader of the Anabaptist movement (Mennonites), agreed with this position. I quote:

"Again, **Children are entitled to the kingdom of heaven, and are under the promise of the grace of God, through Christ; as has been said; and** therefore **we truly believe, that they are blessed, holy and pure, acceptable to God; are under the covenant, and in his church,** but by no means, through any external sign; for there is not a word in all the Scriptures whereby to maintain that children should be admitted into the covenant and the church by such a sign."[1]

---

[1] Menno Simons Complete Works pg 34, Concerning Baptism.

So the Mennonite founder's contention is, essentially, "I understand and agree that infants are in the Church, but I don't see anything actually saying to baptize them." That is a noble, albeit ignorant, stand on the Scriptures. I appreciate his temerity. However, most of his followers have no idea that he ever said that; and none of them, to my knowledge, actually agree with him. As to his assertion that the Scriptures don't contain "a word" about the "external sign"...well, that's patently false. You will see that soon, if you haven't already. Just wait; the best is yet to come.

CAN THEY COME TO JESUS?

Did you notice how Christ made a hard-and-fast rule to allow the children to "come" to Him, and yet the children in Luke 18:15-17 were not coming...they were being *brought*. This shows the passivity of the covenant. These children could, in fact, "come"; but they needed the parents to fulfill the obligation of that command for them. They obey Christ's command to "come" passively; but they are only in obedience to "come" when the parents are in obedience to "bring" them. It's that Federal Headship thing again.[1] If the parent obeys, the infant is obedient. If the parent is disobedient, the infant is considered disobedient as well. That is how God consistently deals with the Church, throughout the Bible. Notice how God deals with babies of the old covenant...

> **He who is eight days old among you shall be circumcised,** every male child in your generations, he who is born in your house or bought with money from any foreigner who is not your descendant. He who is born in your house and he who is bought with your money must be circumcised, and My covenant shall be in your flesh for an everlasting covenant. **And the uncircumcised male child, who is not circumcised in the flesh of his foreskin, that person**

---

[1] See chapter 1.

shall be cut off from his people; he has broken My covenant" (Gen. 17:12-14).

Infants who were not circumcised at *eight days old* were considered covenant-breakers. The infants themselves, *not their parents*, are called covenant-breakers. But how can that be, when the infants have no choice in the matter whatsoever? How can God call a nine-day-old baby a covenant-breaker, when he had nothing to do with it? It's because the infants are *passive* in obedience and disobedience. If the parents broke the covenant, the child was a covenant-breaker, too. Infants have someone appointed to either keep or break the covenant obligations for them: their parents. The child is completely dependent upon the parents to fulfill the covenant obligations for him. Thus, in God's view, the child actually obeys or disobeys; he just does so passively, through the parents.

Baptists have typically rejected the idea that God covenants with our children today, because of the whole "belief" issue. They say that the infants cannot choose to enter into covenant with the Lord, so they cannot be in covenant with the Lord. Once again, they ignore the obvious fact that it is God Himself who chose to covenant with the children of believers in the above text. Not the children, or the parents of the children...only God. If He chose to do it that way with the people in those times, why will He not do it that way with us today? Has He changed His mind about the way He should administer covenants?

In the Apostle Paul's letter to the Philippians, when he argued that he was "circumcised the eighth day," he was clearly making a point in regard to his complete compliance to the law of God.

If anyone else thinks he may have confidence in the flesh, I more so: **circumcised the eighth day,** of the stock of Israel, of the tribe of Benjamin, a Hebrew of the Hebrews; concerning the law, a Pharisee; concerning zeal, persecuting the church; concerning the righteousness which is from the law, blameless (Phil. 3:4-6).

Why would he argue that way? So what if he was circumcised? After all, he was just an infant; so how could it have been held against him if his parents didn't circumcise him? As long as he obeyed after his "age of accountability," he was all right, wasn't he? Of course not. Paul's reason for writing this, was that he wanted to show that he was in obedience to the law of God from birth. And he was only obedient because his *parents* were obedient.

This is extremely important, because Christ Himself had to be circumcised in order to keep the law. It was Mary and Joseph who kept God's law of circumcision for our Lord Jesus. If they had not fulfilled the Child's covenant obligations on His behalf, then you could not be saved, because Jesus would have been a covenant-breaker! He would then have been in our same situation: in need of a Savior. God could not allow that to happen; so He placed His beloved Son in the womb of a virtuous, godly woman, and in the house of a man who would rather die than break covenant with God. In this way, God made sure that Jesus would truly be the Savior, and not in need of one Himself. The Scriptures teach us that God was very concerned about whom He placed His Son with—so much so, that He sent an angel to each parent to explain what He was going to do.

And so I ask all of my Christian Brethren, do you think that your children are an accident? Do you think that God did not care about where He was going to put them? He has placed them in your home because He wanted them brought up as covenant-keepers...or has He? Perhaps He has placed them in your home because He knew that you would *not* raise them to be Christians. Perhaps He placed them there because He knew that you would only take them to church once a week, and neglect to instruct them daily in His holy faith. He knew that you would send them to those pagan government schools that will teach them to abhor anything to do with God. He knew that you would let your child watch all manner of perversions on TV. He knew that you would prefer to see your children have worldly success in business or in a sports team, rather than to be "overly religious." Our God is sovereign. Perhaps it was His judgment on those children for Him to place them in your home.

You tell me: which was it? I assure you, it was a blessing on my children to be born into my house. They may very well abandon their God when they leave my house; but if they do, God will have a hotter place in hell for them, because they spurned the obvious blessings which He bestowed upon them.

GLORIOUS ADOPTION

I have an adopted brother. In normal conversation, I don't refer to him as my *adopted* brother, but simply as *my brother*. However, I'm not afraid to let people know that he's adopted, either. I think that it's a glorious thing that he is my father's son, just as truly as I am my father's son; and it's all because my father decided to make him a part of his family.

Well, it's even more glorious when we are talking about the adoption of a sinner into the family of God. The Scriptures are quite clear: when a sinner is converted to faith in Christ, he is adopted into God's family.[1] Then—and only then—can the convert be counted as a true son of God and brother of Jesus Christ. *Brother* of Jesus Christ—as true as if you were born to Mary and Joseph!

Here's another thought. All of my brother's sons are just as truly my father's grandsons as mine are. When my father adopted my brother, he also adopted all of the future children that my brother would have. Well, God's family is no different. Remember, it wasn't some clever guy who came up with the idea of adoption; it was *God's* idea, and *He* gave the idea to mankind, man didn't just make it up. God's design was that the adopted person actually becomes a son of the adopter, in every sense of the word; and this includes the future children being his as well. Of course, they may reject their family and their family name, if they choose to do so later in life—just like with natural-born children. But they have to reject it.

[1] Romans 8:15, 23; 9:4; Galatians 4:5; Ephesians 1:5.

Is Israel the Church?

Today, many people make an unbiblical distinction between the Church of the New Testament and the Church of the Old Testament; as if they are not one Church that has matured, but are rather two distinct entities. Look at the way in which the New Testament authors thought that Israel was the immature Church...

> This is he who was in the congregation [εκκλησια; Church] in the wilderness with the Angel who spoke to him on Mount Sinai, and with our fathers (Acts 7:38).

This was spoken by Stephen the martyr. He obviously felt that Old Testament Israel was simply the immature "Church" of Jesus Christ, because he actually calls it the "Church in the wilderness."

> And I will establish My covenant between Me and you and your descendants after you in their generations, for an everlasting covenant, to be God to you and your descendants after you (Gen. 17:7).

> And if you are Christ's, then you are Abraham's seed, and heirs according to the promise (Gal. 3:29).

You see, Paul tells us that the promises given to Abraham and his seed also extend to us, who belong to Christ. He does not merely state that we can have whatever is left over from the children of Abraham; instead, he boldly proclaims that we *are* the "seed" of Abraham. You are the heirs of the divine promise that God gave to Abraham. You know what an heir is, don't you? It's someone who inherits something because of *relation*. You have inherited this promise because you belong to Christ, having been adopted into His family through faith. *Your children* inherit the same promise, simply because you have it. But just like you, your children must have faith to keep the covenant with God. If they do not, they are covenant-breakers who need to be "cut off" from among their people. You see, it's no different from Israel. Abraham's children inherited the promise, but they needed to have faith (like their father) in order for the covenant to be kept. If they were unbelievers, then they were cut off from among their people. It's still the same way. Notice how Jeremiah speaks of the Jews being broken off of the tree of the people of God, because they broke covenant with Him.

> What has My beloved to do in My house, having done lewd deeds with many? ... The Lord called your name Green **Olive Tree,** Lovely and of Good Fruit. With the noise of a great tumult He has kindled fire on it, **and its branches are broken.** For the Lord of hosts, who planted you, has pronounced doom against you for the evil of the house of Israel and of the house of Judah (Jer. 11:15-17).

Now compare that to what Paul says in his Epistle to the Romans.

> And if some of **the branches were broken off,** and you, being a wild olive tree, were grafted in among them, and with them became a partaker of the root and fatness of **the olive tree,** do not boast against the branches. But if you do boast, remember that you do not support the root, but the root supports you (Rom. 11:17, 18).

In this passage, Paul clearly completes the thought of Jeremiah's prophecy. Please notice that Paul does not say that one tree is cut down and another planted; but rather, that the wild olive branches are grafted onto the original tree that Jeremiah prophesied about. You see, it has always been the same tree—the same Church, if you will. Only now, it's grown and matured to encompass the Gentiles. So we don't say, "Israel was the people of God at one time, but now the Church is the people of God." Rather, we say, "The Church at one time encompassed only Jews, but now it has been opened up to include Gentiles as well." Read the opening chapters of the book of Acts, and that is the constant theme that you will find there.

Chapter 5

EXAMINING THE EVIDENCE

In this chapter, we will be looking at additional Biblical evidence that supports infant baptism by sprinkling. Some of these evidences, you may have heard before; some, maybe not. But all of these arguments are relevant. The Paedobaptist apologist should be very familiar with them. Since Credobaptists have typically heard some form of these arguments (especially the household baptisms), you should be prepared to point out their erroneous reasoning to them. If you have done your groundwork, this should not be too difficult.

A SIGN OF FAITH GIVEN TO INFANTS?

A classic Credobaptist argument is that baptism is for those who possess faith; therefore, infants are ruled out. While Chapter 2 has already shown how that is not true, you can also point out the following text as another blow to this theory.

> He received the sign of circumcision, a seal of the righteousness of the faith which he had while still uncircumcised (Rom. 4:11).

Please remind the Credobaptist that it is irrelevant whether circumcision was replaced by baptism or not. Even Credobaptists acknowledge that they have parallels, so just keep the discussion about the parallels. Let's notice that this text was referring to Abraham. Abraham had faith, and so the Lord gave him His "seal of the righteousness of faith." God sealed Abraham with circumcision as a sign of the righteousness that he had, due to his faith in God. It's what the text states, so no Credobaptist should have a problem with that. Then, God took that very same seal of the righteousness *of faith,* and gave it to *millions of infants.* The Credobaptist cannot argue that we can't give a sign of faith to infants, because God Himself gave a sign of faith to millions of infants. God *always* works with families; He *always* makes covenants with a person and their *posterity*. It's God who created the family; so of course, God is going to work in relation to the family. It's really that simple. Upon the faith of Abraham, God sealed his sons with the sign of the righteousness of *faith.* Upon *your* faith, God desires to seal your children with the new sign of the righteousness of faith: baptism.

Abraham's faith was a blessing upon his children. Think with me now: at what point did Isaac benefit from the faith of his father Abraham? Was it only when he was old enough to embrace the God of Israel for himself with his own faith? Is that when he inherited the benefits of his father's faith? Did the *infant* Isaac benefit at all from the faith of his father? Yes, of course he did. Isaac would not have even existed, had it not been for the faith of Abraham. *That's a pretty big benefit!* To see more benefits, just compare Isaac with a heathen child. At birth, Isaac inherited the promise of God that was made to his father. No heathen child could claim that. Isaac was nurtured in a godly home where righteousness dwelt, and he never had to be subject to the heathenish human sacrifices of the pagan nations. Heathen children were subject to all sorts of brutality. Isaac was under the protection of God Almighty Himself. No heathen child could claim that.

So was Abraham's faith a blessing for Isaac? Of course it was; and our faith is a blessing to our children, for the same reasons. At birth, *our* children inherited the promise of God that was made to us. No heathen child can claim that. *Our* children are taught righteousness and the fear of the Lord from birth. No heathen child can claim that. *Our* children are nurtured in a godly home where they never will be subject to the heathenish practice of *abortion*. Heathen children are being butchered daily by the hundreds, as mothers desire convenience over children. *Our* children are under the protection of God Almighty Himself. No heathen child can claim that. The great difference between our children and the children of Abraham is that Abraham was faithful to give his children the seal of the righteousness of faith, as God commanded him; and our Baptist brethren have not.

John Calvin concurs with this...

"First, it is certain, that the faith of Abraham was of advantage to his posterity, when he embraced the free covenant offered to him and to his seed. We must hold a similar belief with regard to all believers, that, by their faith, the grace of God is extended to their children and their children's children even before they are born. The same thing takes place in infants who are not yet of such an age as to be capable of faith."[1]

FAITH OF THE PARENTS

Those of the Credobaptist persuasion always tell us that the faith of the parents does nothing for the children in their households. As I've pointed out, Abraham's children benefited greatly by his faith. That's a good point to press home; however, there is much more that can be said about the topic. So let's examine what the New Testament teaches regarding this. Does the faith of a parent benefit the children? We will look at both physical benefits and spiritual benefits.

The following texts make it clear that one parent's faith can reap powerful physical benefits for the child.

Then one of the crowd answered and said, "Teacher, **I brought You my son,** who has a mute spirit. And wherever it seizes him, it throws him down; he foams at the mouth, gnashes his teeth, and becomes rigid...So He asked his father, "How long has this been happening to

---

[1] John Calvin, Harmony of the Evangelists pg 393.

him?" And he said, "**From childhood**. And often he has thrown him both into the fire and into the water to destroy him. But if You can do anything, **have compassion on us and help us**." Jesus said to him, "If **you** can believe, all things are possible to him who believes." Immediately the father of the child cried out and said with tears, "Lord, **I** believe; help **my** unbelief!" When Jesus saw that the people came running together, He rebuked the unclean spirit, saying to it, "Deaf and dumb spirit, I command you, come out of him and enter him no more!" (Mark 9:17-27)

And behold, one of the rulers of the synagogue came, Jairus by name. And when he saw Him, he fell at His feet and begged Him earnestly, saying, "**My little daughter lies at the point of death. Come and lay Your hands on her, that she may be healed, and she will live.**"...Then He took the child by the hand, and said to her, "Talitha, cumi," which is translated, "Little girl, I say to you, arise." Immediately the girl arose and walked, for she was twelve years of age. And they were overcome with great amazement (Mark 5:22, 23, 41, 42).

So Jesus came again to Cana of Galilee where He had made the water wine. And there was a certain nobleman whose son was sick at Capernaum. When he heard that Jesus had come out of Judea into Galilee, **he went to Him and implored Him to come down and heal his son,** for he was at the point of death...The nobleman said to Him, "Sir, come down before my child dies!" Jesus said to him, "**Go your way; your son lives**" (John 4:46-54).

And behold, a woman of Canaan came from that region and cried out to Him, saying, "Have mercy on **me**, O Lord, Son of David! My daughter is severely demon-possessed."...Then Jesus answered and said to her, "O woman, **great is your faith**! Let it be to you as you desire." **And her daughter was healed** from that very hour (Matt. 15:22-28).

In all of these passages, the faith of one parent effected an actual *physical* blessing upon their children. The child's faith is explicitly ruled out from being a source of the healing. So to say that the children of Christians are not benefited by the parent's faith, is foolishness, to put it nicely.

All right, that's all fine and dandy, but what about spiritual blessings? Does my faith as a parent benefit my children spiritually?

> Then **they brought** little children to Him, that He might touch them; but the disciples rebuked those who brought them. But when Jesus saw it, He was greatly displeased and said to them, "Let the little children come to Me, and do not forbid them; for of such is the kingdom of God. Assuredly, I say to you, whoever does not receive the kingdom of God as a little child will by no means enter it." And He took them up in His arms, laid His hands on them, and **blessed** them (Mark 10:13-16).

> Then they also brought infants to Him that He might touch them; but when the disciples saw it, they rebuked them. But Jesus called them to Him and said, "Let the little children come to Me, and do not forbid them; for of such is the kingdom of God (Luke 18:15, 16).

I submit to you that we can still bring our "infants" to our Lord, and He will bless them spiritually. But what exactly does that mean? Well, did Jesus actually convey a blessing on those children or not? The text doesn't say that they were sick and He healed them. He certainly didn't give them money or something. There was no physical blessing. It was spiritual, pure and simple. By the faith of these parents, their children were soundly "in the kingdom." The Lord delights in parents who storm the kingdom of heaven with violence, on behalf of their children. And He rewards them when they do so.

BY FAITH MOSES...

> By faith Moses, when he was born, was hidden three months by his parents, because they saw *he was* a beautiful child; and they were not afraid of the king's command (Hebrews 11:23).

I do agree; this seems like a strange passage with which to support infant baptism. But bear with me a moment, because I want you to see that the Biblical authors actually assumed that the faith of the parents counted as the faith of the child.

Notice that in this entire chapter, the language pattern is always the same. First, we have "By faith (name)." Then it describes what he or she did.

> *Hebrews 11:4:* By faith Abel...
> *verse 5:* By faith Enoch...
> *verse 7:* By faith Noah...
> *verse 8:* By faith Abraham...
> *verse 11:* By faith Sarah...
> *verse 17:* By faith Abraham...
> *verse 20:* By faith Isaac...
> *verse 21:* By faith Jacob...
> *verse 22:* By faith Joseph...
> **verse 23:** By faith Moses, when he was born, was hidden three months by his parents, because they saw *he was* a beautiful child; and they were not afraid of the king's command.
> *verse 24:* By faith Moses...
> *verse 27:* By faith he (Moses)...
> *verse 28:* By faith he (Moses)...
> *verse 29:* By faith they (the Israelites)...
> *verse 31:* By faith the harlot Rahab...

So here in verse 23, for the first time in the middle of all of these "by faith" statements, we have a change that has made it necessary for all of the commentators to explain what they thought was a clear mistake of wording by the author. Why would it say, "By faith Moses," when it was the faith of *Moses' parents* that was under discussion? Some modern translations have even tried to correct the error by changing the word order, rendering it, "By faith Moses' parents..." We can clearly see that it was the parents who hid Moses; Moses didn't hide himself.

Yes; but you see, that's just it! The Greek text does not change the wording; it reads just like it does in the English: "By faith Moses." And the author did not make a mistake; he was simply assuming what every Jew in Biblical times assumed: *the faith of the parents was counted as the faith of the child.* Thus, you could say, "By faith Moses," and then state what his parents did for him. Similarly, you could boast of being circumcised on the eighth day, when it was your parents who did that for you.[1] In the eyes of the Biblical authors, faithful parents equaled faithful children, until the children strayed. Then they were scorned for not following in their parents' ways. But until then, they were counted faithful, just as their parents were faithful.

Households—The Real Argument

Enter into a conversation about baptism with a Credobaptist; and invariably, the household baptisms will come up, even if the Paedobaptist himself doesn't bring them up. The Credobaptist is primed with his answers on those texts, and so he can't help bringing them up. He loves to tell you that these households didn't contain any infants, and that these households were only made up of persons who were old enough to express personal faith in Christ; and you can't prove otherwise! Of course, it's impossible to know if there really were infants in these households at all. But why do you think that the Credobaptists are so eager to show the impossible? Isn't it clear that they know very well that they give everyone the impression that infants were baptized right along with the adults? They do know it; so they spend an inordinate amount of time trying to convince themselves that the households couldn't possibly have contained any infants.

Unfortunately, many Paedobaptist apologists are too quick to give up this ground and essentially say, "We can't prove they were there, and you can't prove they weren't; so let's move on to other issues." Whoa! Stop the press! Don't give up the high ground! The

---

[1] Philippians 3:5.

Credobaptists already *know* that *household* means what it means, and they are trying to suppress that knowledge because of their presuppositions. Your job is simply to get them to acknowledge it, and to remove that presupposition. Don't get bogged down with the side issues; make the Credobaptist struggle with the real issues regarding the household baptisms.

So let's start by taking a look at a verse or two from 1 Corinthians 16.

> Now I urge you, brothers—you know that the household of Stephanas were the first converts in Achaia, and that they have devoted themselves to the service of the saints—be subject to such as these, and to every fellow worker and laborer (1 Cor. 16: 15, 16).

Now, let's apply this to our modern lives. If somebody told you that "the Camp household has devoted themselves to the service of the Lord," would anyone think it strange to find out later that I have an infant child in my house? Of course not. When it is said that the "Camp household has devoted themselves to the service of the Lord," everyone understands that it means that the parents have devoted their family to the service of the Lord, and that they direct their children how to serve Him. It does not necessarily mean that everyone in my family has to be in total, or even substantial, agreement with me. What if I had some opposition from my children between the ages of 10 and 15, because they are particularly shy and don't like to speak to strangers? They still obey me; and they help in some capacity as I, the father, see fit; but they aren't 100% on-board. So would it be wrong, then, to state that the "Camp household has devoted themselves"? Nope. Nobody has any trouble with that in real life. Nobody would stop the person who made that statement, and say, "No; you see, Andrew has an infant and a 2-year-old, so it's incorrect to say that his *household* has devoted themselves to the service of the Lord. It would be more correct to say that *Andrew Camp and his wife and four of his six kids* have devoted themselves..." That would be ridiculous.

In the same way, nobody would have any issue putting infants in Stephanas' household when it says that they "devoted themselves to the service of the saints." If I asked anyone whether it would matter to them that Stephanas had an infant child along with his other eight children, they wouldn't bat an eye. After all, that's what you get in "households." But then, we read this verse from 1 Corinthians 1:

> I did baptize also the household of Stephanas. Beyond that, I do not know whether I baptized anyone else (1 Cor. 1:16).

Now we have a problem, don't we? Here at this point, no Credobaptist wants to admit infants into Stephanas' household—all because we introduced something that, according to Baptist theory, is not supposed to be for infants. It's a pre-conceived theology that is getting in the way of what the Bible actually teaches.

Of course, Scripture is the best interpreter of Scripture. We all know that (or at least, we should). The only way in which someone can approach the New Testament "household" texts and believe that infants are *not* to be baptized, is by suppressing the knowledge that they already have. They know very well that the term *household* would include infants *if there were any there;* so according to their pre-conceived notions, they must play the ridiculous game of proving that infants *were not in the households* that were mentioned. They know something is not right about what they are trying to say; but they know it *must be* right, because that's what the Bible is *supposed* to teach, right?

I feel silly even having to do this; but some Credobaptists will not let this go unless it's specifically shown to them that the Bible does indeed define the term *household*. So, there is a story in the book of Numbers that clearly and explicitly includes "little children" in the term *household*. Remember, this is not just the English definition of the term, but this is the way that Scripture itself defines the term *household*. Notice:

> So they got away from around the tents of Korah, Dathan, and Abiram; and Dathan and Abiram came out and stood at the door of their tent,

with their wives, their sons, and **their little children** (Num. 16:27).

And just a few verses down...

And the earth opened its mouth and swallowed them up, with **their households** and all the men with Korah, with all their goods (Num. 16: 32).

The "households" of Dathan and Abiram included "little children." And even in God's judgment, He included the children under the fathers' federal headship. Now you have a clear Scriptural example to prove to the Credobaptist what he knew was true all along. The term *household* refers to all who are in the house, including infants if they are there.

But there is one more thing in this passage that raises a really solid point. Not only does this passage specifically put "little children" inside the Biblical *household,* but it also specifically puts "wives" and "sons" in the Biblical *household.* Why is this obvious fact so important? Well, our Credobaptist brethren constantly bring up the fact that infants are not specifically mentioned in the household baptisms recorded for us in the book of Acts. Well, are the wives specifically mentioned? How about daughters? Sons? You can't prove that any wives were present in those households, either; nor any other category of persons. So does that mean that they weren't there? This is the absurdity that the Credobaptist position leaves you with. In actuality, all of those categories of persons are mentioned in the one word *household.* The inspired writer didn't need to mention wives or sons or daughters or infants; all of those categories are summed up in the one term *household.* Anybody within that term who happened to be there, was included in it.

Thus, because of the household baptisms recorded for us in the Bible, you will have to believe that infants were baptized in the early church (as the church fathers attest for us). Otherwise, you will have to believe that the New Testament authors meant to deceive us by their very use of the word *household.* If neither of those is the case, then they made a grievous mistake by not qualifying their language, and they have thereby plunged the Church into needless debates. To accept the Baptist position, you have to believe that Luke *was inspired* to use the word *household,* not only differently from the common everyday usage of then and now, but also differently from the meaning given to it in the *inspired* Old Testament Scriptures.

Why would Luke even use the word *household?* Why didn't Luke just use other words if he meant to convey that no infants were baptized? Why didn't he just say, "And all of the adults in the house were baptized"? Or easier yet, "And all those in the household who expressed belief..."? That would have been very easy, but the Holy Spirit certainly doesn't want this division in the Church. Why would Luke choose a word that *universally* includes infants *if they are there,* and is explicitly used in the Old Testament to include infants? The meaning of the word is so obvious, that we have the same meaning today.[1] Was Luke trying to confuse us? Or did he understand that word in the exact same way that the other Biblical authors understood it? Why would God *inspire* Luke to use the term *household,* when He didn't mean to convey the same meaning that He Himself had assigned to it elsewhere in His Word?

Now, I concede without reservation that there are some households that *do not* contain infants. I will also concede that the households referred to in these New Testament texts may not, in fact, have contained infants.[2] Indeed, they may have been households in which all of the infants were grown. *But that is not the point.* The term "household" *universally* includes infants *if they are there.* Therefore, Luke could *not* have meant to convey that *only* adults *could* be baptized. If Luke had meant to convey that only adults could be baptized, either he chose the wrong term, or else he failed to accurately convey his meaning by adding the phrase "except for the

---

[1] Household – "The members of a family and others living under the same roof." Websters II dictionary.

[2] With household baptisms being so prevalent in a short history like the book of Acts, one could come to the conclusion that many more household baptisms actually took place. So it would be a stretch to try to say that infants were *never* included in *any* of the household baptisms that took place.

infants." We who believe in the inspiration of Scripture know that neither of these is an option. *Anyone reading that term, since it was first written until now, would believe that it includes infants if they were there; unless, of course, their pre-conceived theology does not fit with the Biblical meaning of that word; then they simply re-define the word and destroy the integrity of Scripture.*

Allow me to illustrate. Imagine the local government in a rural community warning that there was a sheep rustler going around, so you should "make sure you have your flocks branded." All right, so you go down to your neighbor Joe's, and you see him branding his flock because he's afraid of his sheep getting stolen. You notice that there are no lambs in his flock. Then you go to Sam's house, and he's also branding his sheep; but he has no lambs in his flock, either. So you go home to brand your flock, but you do have lambs. Based on the absence of lambs in your neighbors' flocks, would you judge that lambs are not fit recipients of branding? So, *who cares* if Lydia didn't have any infants in her household! The Holy Spirit inspired the record of whole households being baptized, so whole households are fit recipients of baptism. Of course, the exception in the example of branding the flocks would be if the said government warning contained a caveat: "But don't brand lambs under two months of age, as it may be dangerous to their health," or some other such thing. However, we have no such caveat from the inspired pen of Luke; therefore, language itself demands the fact that Luke thought infants were *fit recipients* of baptism.

To speak about "flock branding" without caveat, would clearly indicate to every sane person that lambs were fit recipients of said branding. The very phrase "household baptism" demands the same interpretation. Everyone knows that if you say the word *household,* you mean to convey that even infants can be included. So Joshua said, "As for me and my house..." Hmmm. I don't know about that one... Did Joshua really mean his *entire* household? Or just the members of his household that were old enough to agree with ol' Dad? Did he take a vote? Nope; Joshua was man enough to say, "If I am going to follow the Lord, so will my children...even my infants." When Luke wrote "you and your household" by the inspiration of the Holy Spirit, he didn't mean anything other than the standard meaning of the word *household*.

Given the number of baptisms found in the book of Acts, and the number of them that were household baptisms, I would expect as much to see them take place today. I have witnessed household baptisms. And both of the household baptisms that I saw, included infants. Ask your Credobaptist friend how many "household baptisms" he has seen. How many households has he seen converted and baptized, all at the same time? I never saw one when I was a Baptist. But then again, I wouldn't expect to, because they don't follow the New Testament pattern.

I like to argue further with my Credobaptist brethren in this fashion. The qualifications for elders in the Church include the stipulation that they must be...

> ...one who rules his own **house** well, having his children in submission with all reverence (for if a man does not know how to rule his own **house**, how will he take care of the church of God?) (1 Tim. 3:4, 5).

In addition, they must be...

> ...the husband of one wife, having faithful children not accused of dissipation or insubordination (Tit. 1:6).

The text says, "rules his own **house** well." Remind your Credobaptist friend that the word here is the same as the word describing household baptisms; and then ask if this statement would carry the same meaning, with or without the presence of infants in the potential elder's household. He should have no problem saying yes. Then proceed to tell him that if he was consistent, the elders in the Church would not be allowed to have infants in their households. Why? Because no infant can be in "submission with all reverence." If an infant can't do that, then of course, elders are not supposed to have infant children. Sound familiar?

THE EXAMPLE THEY ARE LOOKING FOR . . .

As stated elsewhere in this book, I don't agree with any of the Credobaptists' contentions about infant baptism, one of which is that there is no *command* to baptize them. Another is that there is no *example* in Scripture for the practice. Both are flat-out wrong. I have already shown that baptism by sprinkling of entire households, including infants, occurred as often as death occurred. So in New Testament Israel, people were used to seeing infants baptized, along with the rest of the household. I have also already shown how household baptisms, while not explicitly mentioning infants, prove that the Apostles and the Holy Spirit meant that they, too, should be partakers of baptism. Now we will look at additional instances of both an example and a command to baptize infants.

Let's start with yet another explicit example in Scripture that proves, beyond a reasonable doubt, that infants were indeed baptized.

> Moreover, brethren, I do not want you to be unaware that **all our fathers** were under the cloud, **all passed through the** sea, **all were baptized** into Moses in the cloud and in the sea, **all ate** the same spiritual food, **all drank** the same spiritual drink. For they drank of that spiritual Rock that followed them, and that Rock was Christ (1 Cor. 10:1, 2).

Here, the Apostle Paul is clearly drawing parallels from the Old Testament to compare with Christian baptism and the Lord's Supper. He goes on to say that even though "our fathers"[1] partook of "baptism" and the "spiritual food," many of them still perished. And so the Apostle warns us that this could happen to us as well, even though we are baptized and partake of the "spiritual food" of the Lord's Supper. His warning is clear: we are not to presume upon the sacraments; we must only look at our obedience for assurance. If you

---

[1] Notice that Paul is speaking to the Corinthian Church—full of Gentile believers—yet they are still referred to as "our fathers." See – Is Israel the Church?

are not obedient to God, you have broken the covenant that the sacraments represent; and so you should not presume upon them for a feeling of security.

So the Apostle Paul says that all of our fathers went through a ceremony that was similar to what we have today; they were all baptized. But wait a minute—how many of the "fathers" were just infants at the time of the Exodus? There could have been *thousands*. Would anyone argue that *no* infants passed through the Red Sea? Of course not. So here is a definitive proof that infants were indeed *baptized*. Oh, but you know how a Credobaptist would want to respond, don't you? "That isn't *real* baptism." Right? However, the Apostle Paul thought that this baptism was equivalent to ours, just like he felt that their eating and drinking the "spiritual food" and water were equivalent to our partaking of the Lord's Supper. So if you wish to argue that those infants that passed through the Red Sea were not *really* baptized, you will have to also argue that they did not *really* partake of spiritual food. According to Paul, both were as real as our current sacraments.

Let me be really clear here. I am contending that the Apostle Paul clearly intended to link this "baptism" and our current "baptism" as being, in essence, the same. In the first "baptism," there were perhaps thousands of infants and little children. If the Apostle Paul knew of some reason that infants should not be baptized, this would have been a good time to proclaim it. As a matter of fact, if Paul did not intend for the presence of children to be included at the time of the Exodus, he surely was sloppy in comparing baptism to such an event. After all, the Holy Spirit-inspired Scriptures make a clear emphasis on the fact that children were indeed present during the Exodus, and that they were an integral part of the people of God. Furthermore, Moses had to specifically instruct Pharaoh that all of the children had to leave Egypt, as well as the adults. The Holy Scriptures *stress* the fact that infants were included in the Exodus.[1] Thus it would be sloppy exegesis for Paul to use the Exodus as an

---

[1] Exodus 10:8-11, 24; 1 Corinthians 10:1.

illustration of baptism, if he intended to exclude infants from being baptized.

The Command They Are Looking For...

Now, on to the specific command to baptize our children.

> Go therefore and make disciples of all the nations, baptizing them in the name of the Father and of the Son and of the Holy Spirit, teaching them to observe all things that I have commanded you; and lo, I am with you always, even to the end of the age (Matt. 28:19, 20).

In this passage, Christ Himself gives us three commands:

1. *Make disciples of all nations.*
2. *Baptize them in the name of the triune God.*
3. *Teach them to obey.*

Everybody can see that those commands are clearly spelled out. We don't need to quibble with Credobaptists over whether or not this is a command to "baptize the nations," or any other such silliness. Focus on the facts. This is the only command in Scripture which specifically states the persons who are to be baptized by the Apostles, and they are all included in the category of *disciple*. Now point out to your Credobaptist friend that his or her children *are disciples* of Christ. A disciple is a *student*. Are you a student of Christ? If so, are you not teaching your children *from infancy* to follow Christ? Then they are disciples of Christ as well. According to the Bible, whatever the father is, the children are as well. Thus, if I am a Muslim, my children are Muslims as well; if I am a pagan, my children are pagans as well; if I am a Jew, my children are Jewish as well; and if I am a

Christian, my children are most definitely Christians as well. That's why the children of pagans were put to death as well as the adults.[1]

More to the point, when I share this passage with a Baptist, the consistent answer that I get is, "My children are not disciples." At this point, I like to shock the person I'm speaking with, by making the following statement: "If your children are not disciples, *then neither are you.*" When they show their shock, I simply ask them if they are obeying the command of the eternal Word of God, and bringing up their children "in the training and admonition of the Lord."[2] To this, they invariably answer in the affirmative. "There you have it!" I exclaim. "They are disciples...and so are you...congratulations!"

So, according to the divine command of Matthew 28, you *must* baptize your little disciples of Christ. It's really that simple.

Do not let a Credobaptist get out from under this clearly Biblical doctrine. How is it possible for a child to be instructed by and obey someone, and yet not be that person's disciple? And if that could be possible, what are they called before they actually do become that person's disciple? A learner? Nope, that means the same thing. Umm, a student? Nope, same thing. How about a proselyte? I don't quite know what that means...but I think it's the same thing... At what point do they actually become a *disciple?* Is there a certain amount of learning that needs to take place in order to become a disciple? If so, how much? It seems to me that the first day a student sits in class, he is a disciple of the teacher, before that teacher even opens his or her mouth. Now, later on, he may reject everything that his teacher taught him; but who would ever suggest that he was never a disciple of that teacher? Aristotle eventually rejected Plato's Rationalism in favor of his own Empirical methodology, but does

---

[1] It is amazing how the Baptist viewpoint is in complete agreement with atheists on this subject. In his book *The God Delusion,* as well as in interviews, Richard Dawkins argues that it is absurd and wrong for anyone to call a child a "Christian," if the child is too young to make up his own mind.   The individualistic and autonomous mindset of the atheist is clearly seen in Credobaptist theology.

[2] Ephesians 6:4.

that mean that he was never Plato's disciple? He learned from him; therefore, he was his disciple.

All right, all right; enough speculation. What does the Bible say concerning the question of when our children are disciples?

I think that David would have a really hard time with someone telling him that he was not a disciple of Christ from birth.

> Yet you are he who took me from the womb; **you made me trust you at my mother's breasts. On you was I cast from my birth,** and **from my mother's womb you have been my God** (Ps. 22:9, 10).

Is that not true of our children? Has the Lord Jesus been their God from their "mother's womb"? Oblige the Credobaptist to explain why that is not so.

What about Isaiah?

> Listen, O coastlands, to Me, And take heed, you peoples from afar! **The LORD has called Me from the womb;** From the matrix of My mother He has made mention of My name. And He has made My mouth like a sharp sword; In the shadow of His hand He has hidden Me, And made Me a polished shaft; In His quiver He has hidden Me (Isa. 49:1, 2).

> And now the LORD says, **Who formed Me from the womb to be His Servant,** To bring Jacob back to Him, So that Israel is gathered to Him (For I shall be glorious in the eyes of the LORD, And My God shall be My strength) (Isa. 49:5).

A servant from the womb? How can that be? I thought being a servant was something that you chose to do.

Jeremiah, anyone?

> **Before I formed you in the womb I knew you;** Before you were born I sanctified you; I ordained you a prophet to the nations (Jer. 1:5).

Ordained to be a "prophet" before he was born. Wow! And the poor Credobaptist children can't even be thought of as learners of Christ?

I can hear the Credobaptist now... "Oh Andrew, you don't understand. Those examples are in the Old Testament. Things are different now." Really? We have already discussed this passage; but lest you forget, Paul said of Timothy, "From infancy you have known the holy Scriptures."

Now, consider this also: if a child is part of the kingdom of God (which I have shown to be the case in Chapter 4), then how can they not be a disciple? Aren't only disciples in the kingdom of God?

Challenge your Credobaptist friend with this. Point out that it is absolutely *IMPOSSIBLE* for a child in a Christian home to *NOT* be a disciple of Christ.[1] The reason why it's impossible is because Christians will obey the command of God to "bring them up in the training and admonition of the Lord." *By default,* they are disciples of Christ. If they are not brought up in that training, it's because they were not reared in a Christian home. "If your children are not disciples of Christ, *then neither are you.*" Harsh? Yes, but it gets the point across. If a child is not brought up as a disciple of Christ, it is because he has unbelieving parents. Happily, most of our Credobaptist brethren *do* bring them up as disciples of Christ, even though they deny it. They have just been misled by the very Baptist doctrine that they are so fond of.

So a disciple is a student. It's that simple. A disciple is someone who still must learn to obey, and Christ commands us to teach them to obey. But first, He commands us to baptize them. He does not command us to withhold baptism from them until the time when we have taught them to obey. On the contrary, we are to baptize them simply on the basis of their being disciples. The Apostle Paul

---

[1] In light of this, I find myself in complete agreement with Wayne Grudem when he claims, "The outward symbol of beginning the Christian life should only be given to those who show evidence of having begun the Christian life." Systematic Theology pg 970. Being born in my house is evidence that my children have begun the Christian life.

also tells us to teach our children to obey. That's because Paul recognized that your children are disciples, and he assumed that they had been baptized.

Why didn't Philip tell the Ethiopian eunuch that he needed to be catechized prior to his baptism? Why did Paul not go to learn from the other Apostles before his baptism? Why did all of the baptisms of the New Testament happen immediately upon conversion? It was because, no matter how ignorant they were at the time, they became disciples at that point. Even Ananias and Sapphira. Even Simon Magus. They were all disciples of Christ, so they were baptized. THEN they were taught to obey...or not.

Another persuasive argument to give to a Credobaptist in this train of thought, is to change the command. If the command that Jesus gave was, "Go therefore and make disciples of all the nations, *circumcising* them in the name of the Father and of the Son and of the Holy Spirit, teaching them to observe all things that I have commanded you," then there would be no doubt as to whether or not children were included in the New Covenant. It wouldn't even be debated. As a matter of fact, we see all through the New Testament that they assumed that children were in the New Covenant. How do I know that? Because of all the talk of circumcision. Why did all of those Judaizers bother the early church with the requirement to be circumcised, when circumcision was given 99.9% of the time to infants? Why didn't the Apostles just say, "Hey, children aren't in the covenant people anymore, so away with this circumcision stuff!" No; instead, what you find is controversy and constant trouble, which the Church would not have had if the Apostles had just come out and said that infants no longer count as covenant members, and that the fathers are no longer heads of their households, responsible for their infant members. What we do find, however, is that the Apostles had to explain why we do not need that bloody rite of circumcision for our infants anymore.

Well, just as people would have assumed that children were included if Jesus had commanded to *circumcise* the disciples; the people of that era assumed that children were included when Jesus said to *baptize* them, because they were used to seeing all the members of the household get baptized. And they knew that if the head of the house was a disciple, the rest of the family were disciples as well. It was impossible to be otherwise.

The Heritage of the Servants of the Lord

In Isaiah 54:11-17, the Lord describes what the "heritage of the servants of the Lord" would look like.

> "This is the heritage of the servants of the LORD, And their righteousness is from Me," Says the LORD.

He describes His blessings as decorating our surroundings with beautiful gemstones: "I will lay your stones with colorful gems, And lay your foundations with sapphires. I will make your pinnacles of rubies, Your gates of crystal, And all your walls of precious stones" (verses 11, 12). He says that anyone who assembles against us will fall (verse 15). He says that no weapon that is formed against us shall prosper (verse 17); that we shall not fear (verse 14); and that we shall be established in righteousness (verse 14), because our "'righteousness is from Me,' Says the LORD" (verse 17). These are all very beautiful things, and I am glad that they are included in the "heritage of the servants of the Lord." But one very important aspect of this "heritage" that we, as "servants of the Lord," get to share in, is that all of our "children shall be taught by the Lord" (verse 13). You need to get this across to your Credobaptist brother.

> All your children shall be taught by the LORD, And great shall be the peace of your children.

They shall be the Lord's *disciples,* just as the parents are. So ask your brother again, "Are you a servant of the Lord?" If he answers positively (hopefully, he will), then the word of God promises that his children *are* disciples of the Lord as well as himself.

Disciples Alone?

Fred Malone wrote a book on baptism from the Credobaptist persuasion; perhaps you have seen it. It's called *The Baptism of Disciples Alone*. I could have used that title for my book, and I would have had no problem doing it. I heartily agree that baptism is for "disciples alone"; but unfortunately, *Mr. Malone doesn't.* His book should be called *The Baptism of **Self-aware, Willful** Disciples Alone*, since that is the way he defines the term. In an attempt to prove his point, he says:

> "Every use of the word *disciple* in the New Testament refers to a self-aware, willful follower of a teacher. Therefore, in the Great Commission, Christ defined the subjects of baptism and Christian teaching as self-aware disciples."[1]

First of all, I will give him the benefit of the doubt; and I will assume that he meant to say, "Every *OTHER* use of the word *disciple* in the New Testament refers to a self-aware, willful follower of a teacher." Otherwise, he would be contradicting himself; because if "*every* use of the word *disciple* in the New Testament" referred to "a self-aware, willful follower of a teacher," then why does he need those other texts to support his understanding of the Great Commission? Isn't the Great Commission in Matthew? And isn't that in the New Testament? So if "every use of the word *disciple* in the New Testament refers to a self-aware, willful follower of a teacher," then this one certainly does as well…except it doesn't—which, of course, is why he uses the other Scriptures to support his theory. So let's deal with what he actually meant to say. I will give an alternative example, using the term *teacher* instead.

Every *other* use of the word *teacher* in the New Testament refers to a teacher of religious truth. Therefore, in Romans 2:20, when

---

[1] The Baptism of Disciples Alone. Fred Malone, Pg 159.

Paul refers to "a teacher of babes," "babes" are obviously being taught religion; and thus, the "babes" are *disciples* who must be baptized. Would Mr. Malone agree with this use of his logic?

All right, I will admit that there actually is one verse that doesn't define the word *teacher* as a teacher of religious truth. In Luke 6:40, the term *teacher* could be used for a teacher of *anything,* not just religious truth.

> A disciple is not above his teacher, but everyone who is perfectly trained will be like his teacher (Luke 6:40).

So in this case, the word *teacher* does not *have to* refer to a teacher of religious truth. It could be a teacher of *anything.* But uh-oh, the word *disciple* is in the same boat. It does not mean a "self-aware, willful follower of a teacher," either. It simply means "a learner." This verse could be applied to a child learning to eat with a spoon instead of his hand. The child is still a *disciple,* and the teacher is still a *teacher.* And the text is perfectly applicable to both. It could refer to a mother teaching her child to say "Mama" for the first time, a farmer teaching his hired hand how to pick cotton, or a draftee being instructed how to shoot a rifle. *Willful* or not, it's still a *disciple-teacher* relationship. The fact that every other New Testament text in which the word *teacher* is used, refers to a religious teacher, does not mean that this verse *must* mean the same thing. If you applied that logic to every word in the New Testament, you would have quite a mess on your hands. And of course, the same is true for the term *disciple.* This is purely a weak attempt to get around the obvious fact that infants born into Christian homes are, by default, *disciples of Christ.* The term *disciple* means *learner,* and nothing more. The same thing it means today.

And actually, to the contrary of what Mr. Malone espouses, there are many verses using the term *disciple* that do not refer, or at least, do not *have to* refer, to "self-aware, willful followers" of a teacher. Rather, they can easily be referring to learners of the Christian faith, no matter what age they are; or to a specific people referred to as *disciples.*[1] In many instances, the word *disciple* is a synonym for the word "Church"[2]. One text in particular comes as close as you can get to referring directly to infants; the "yoke on the neck of the *disciples*" was the "yoke" of *circumcision.*

So I conclude that Mr. Malone's attempted definition of *disciple* as "a self-aware, willful follower of a teacher," is flawed from the get-go; but it is a valiant attempt to evade the obvious conclusion: the word *disciple* means *learner.* Sorry, Mr. Malone.

---

[1] In each one of these texts below the term *disciple* can refer to an individual of any age or to a group made up of all ages.

*It is enough for a **disciple** that he be like his teacher, and a servant like his master. If they have called the master of the house Beelzebub, how much more will they call those of his household! (Matt. 10:25)*

*And whoever gives one of these little ones only a cup of cold water in the name of a **disciple**, assuredly, I say to you, he shall by no means lose his reward (Matt. 10:42).*

*Then Saul, still breathing threats and murder against the **disciples** of the Lord, went to the high priest (Acts 9:1).*

*So when he had received food, he was strengthened. Then Saul spent some days with the **disciples** at Damascus (Acts 9:19).*

*And when he had found him, he brought him to Antioch. So it was that for a whole year they assembled with the church and taught a great many people. And the **disciples** were first called Christians in Antioch (Acts 11:26).*

*Now therefore, why do you test God by putting a yoke on the neck of the **disciples** which neither our fathers nor we were able to bear? (Acts 15:10)*

*Now on the first day of the week, when the **disciples** came together to break bread, Paul, ready to depart the next day, spoke to them and continued his message until midnight (Acts 20:7).*

[2] It's funny to sit in a Baptist church (which I often do) and hear them talk of the "church" as if it includes the children as well. "There will be a church picnic this Saturday," etc. Do they intend for the children to stay at home? This just shows that they cannot live within their own theological paradigm. It's not a workable system. They still sing "Jesus loves me" with their supposedly unsaved children.

The Church is a School

Everyone in the Church is a *learner* or *disciple*. We are being *taught* to obey (Matt. 28:19, 20), taught to love each other (1 Thess. 4:9), taught doctrine (2 Thess. 2:15), taught the faith (Col. 2:7), and taught the Word (Gal. 6:6). Taught, taught, taught; teach, teach, teach... I do not need to prove the extent to which the Word of God stresses *teaching* in His Church. We are all enrolled in a School.

No teacher teaches just any person they see, or any child they see. The teacher teaches those who have been enrolled in his or her school. Now, there are two ways to be enrolled in the teacher's school. A grown person can enroll him- or her-*self, or* a child can be enrolled by a parent. Either way, they are still enrolled and considered a student, a learner, and a disciple of the teacher of that school. Although this is true, none of the students (whether enrolled as adults or by their parents) are guaranteed to graduate. Some may "walk with the teacher no more" (John 6:66). Either way, they are still legitimate disciples of that teacher, and they are legitimately enrolled in that school. Now, if the way to enrol in that school was to "fill out a form," would you then believe that my child cannot be enrolled because he cannot yet "fill out a form"? Of course not; you would expect me, as the parent, to fill it out for my child. Do you see how Credobaptists can't follow their own theological paradigm in the real world?

Chapter 6

CHALLENGING THE CREDOBAPTISTS

In this chapter, we are going to look at some additional glaring examples of the inconsistency of the Credobaptist position. We will also examine some more of the minutia, such as the self-washings and the baptism of Namaan.

A LIVING PURGATORY?

Credobaptist theology refers to our children as unbelievers who are outside the Church. According to this mindset, they must come to a point in their lives where they make a "decision" for Christ, just like every other heathen in the world. They must be converted, because they are non-Christians prior to that time.[1]

Do you realize what that means? If our children are not Christians, then they are heathens. If they do not belong to Christ, then they belong to Satan. There are *no half-ways*. The Credobaptist tries to get around this by saying that their children are "dedicated" to God. This intermediate state that Baptists appear to put their children into, reminds me of the Roman Catholic doctrine of Purgatory. You're not in heaven, but you're not in hell either; you're in *purgatory*. Credobaptists are basically placing their children in a

---

[1] Sadly, I cannot lump Baptists into this theology without mentioning that there are also some poor theologians in the Presbyterian and Reformed world, who will espouse this teaching.

living purgatory. They say they aren't Christians, but they aren't heathens either. Well, guess what? Just as there is no Roman Catholic purgatory, there is also no such thing as the living purgatory that Baptists have placed their children in. They are either servants of Christ, or they are servants of Satan. It's that simple. There is absolutely *no neutrality.*

If you want to say that children are indeed heathens, then we must ask this question: on what Scriptural authority do you pray with your heathen children to *your* God? Aren't they supposed to be converted first? You *do* pray with your children, don't you? Don't you conclude your prayers with, "In the name of *our* Savior, Jesus Christ"? Would you pray that with a heathen? The Lord despises their prayers (Prov. 28:9; Ps. 66:18). But you *will* continue to pray that way with your children, because *you know* in your heart of hearts that your children are somehow different from the heathen. Well, they *are* different. They are holy; God has claimed them for Himself. That makes your children *very* different.

This leads me to another point. Many Baptists do realize that there is something very different between their children and heathen children, and yet they believe that they should not be baptized because "the Bible doesn't command us to baptize them." So what do they do? In an amazing show of inconsistency, the Baptist completely makes up his own extra-Biblical ceremony, so that he can feel good about his contradictory theology. He has a baby "dedication" ceremony. There is no Biblical command for such a ceremony; and yet Baptists will rejoice in doing it while they reject baptism for their children, because they believe that there is *no Biblical command* to baptize their children. How does that work?

Another example of the inconsistency of the Baptist position is their wishy-washy view of faith. They say, "Faith is the absolute pre-requisite to baptism." When pressed, the Baptist would lay down his life for that doctrinal stance. When a Paedobaptist claims, "Infants can be baptized without faith," the Baptist will harangue on him for destroying this pre-requisite to baptism. Then, in an amazing turn of events, the Baptist will also say, "Faith is the absolute pre-requisite for salvation." Ask your Baptist brother this question: "Is faith really, absolutely, without exception, the required pre-requisite for salvation?" All right then; what happens to our infants who die? Do they go to hell because they did not have faith? You see, in a marvelous display of inconsistency, the Baptist will balk and say, "Well, no; in the case of infants, they cannot have faith; and so God saves them without it." Which is it?

We Paedobaptists do not baptize people on the grounds of their faith in Christ, and so we do not have the supposed problem that Credobaptists say we have. We baptize people only and always on the basis of their covenantal relationship with God. Has God given His covenant promise to a person or not? That is the question. If He has, then baptize him. If He hasn't, then don't.

So how do we know to whom God has given His covenantal promise? The Bible gives us two ways of knowing. First, by a confession of personal faith in Christ, with a life that backs it up. Second, by being the child of someone who has personal faith in Christ with a life that backs it up. In either case, God has given His covenantal promise to that person, and He commands that we seal that person as belonging to God. We do so through baptism. Can you see the tremendous responsibility that Christian parents have? God has not simply bidden us to do the best we can, in order to influence these children to "get on God's side" someday. It's much more important than that. God has given us children that *He has claimed for Himself.* We need to make sure that those children *serve Him*; it's *our* responsibility if they don't. That's right; it's your fault if your children reject God. We don't like to hear that, but it's true (Prov. 22:6); the responsibility lies squarely on the parents. That is why God bids us to "bring them up in the training and admonition of the Lord" (Eph. 6:4). It's not a choice that the children are left with; it's your responsibility to raise your children *as Christ's.*

"Ye must be born again."

Most Baptists can remember when they made a conscious decision to follow Jesus Christ. Some of them have a story to tell about their conversion experience. I myself have a conversion story. I can tell you about the way in which the Scriptures convicted me of my sins; and how, with much emotion and flare, I left my heathenish ways, repented of my sins, and believed on the Lord Jesus Christ. It wasn't until later that I heard of people who had never had the same experience that I had. They called themselves Christians, they acted like Christians (many times better than myself), and they could not remember a time when they were not Christians. Cynically, I thought that they must not be Christians because they had never had an experience like mine. "They are just fooling themselves," I thought. "They need to get born again!" However, they were living Christ-like lives, and I was not. Imagine my predicament. How was it that these "heathens"—who had no "conversion experiences"—were more holy than me, who did have one? Well, it turns out that they grew up in pious Christian homes; they were taught the Bible from birth; every day, they had family worship; and every day, they were taught to reverence their God. They grew up belonging to God, loving Him, knowing Him, and serving Him. They grew up knowing that Jesus died on the cross for their sins; and that, apart from Him, they had no hope of ever going to heaven. And they never had a conversion "experience!" My friends, that should be the norm—all of our children should grow up like that! That is God's mandate.

I have heard many a Baptist, after hearing a stirring sermon, say something to the effect of, "I feel like I have been born again...*again!*" Do you know what that means? It is an admission that they have just had the same sort of emotional experience that they had when they first "believed." Children who grow up in Baptist homes are given mixed signals. On the one hand, they are told that Jesus is their Savior, that He died for them, that God has blessed them, and that He is their God. And then they are told that they are not Christians. Go figure. These children are told that they will someday have some esoteric experience that will make them Christians; and all the while, the child already trusts in Christ! If you ask these children, they will tell you, "Yes, I trust in Jesus; yes, I love Jesus; yes, I believe in Jesus." But the parents tell them, "You're not a Christian yet, because you haven't had this *experience*." So now the children (who already trust in Christ) look for that feeling that they will get when they finally "give their lives to Christ"; when in reality, they already love Christ and desire to follow Him.[1] Let me randomly ask the children in any pious Baptist Christian home, "Do you trust in Jesus for your salvation?" And I guarantee you that they will answer in one of two ways. They will either answer with a resounding "Yes!" Or (in the rarity) they will say, "I don't know." If they answer with the latter, it is because their parents have taught them that it's some mysterious thing to give their lives to Christ, and they haven't had anything mysterious happen to them. It's a big mess. But if I ask the same children, "Do you love Jesus?" what do you think they will say? I've done the experiment, and haven't yet found one Christian parent who has not taught their child to love Jesus.

But contrary to this *experiential* philosophy, Christ tells us to "follow Me." He never gives us any hint that we are going to go through some mystical event that will make us follow Him. He just bids us to follow Him. And when He tells us how to know if we or others are truly Christians, He doesn't tell us to ask them, "Have you had your new birth, brother?" or, "Have you been converted?" He simply bids us to know them "by their fruit." Obedience—that is how we are to tell if someone is "safely in the fold"; their *obedience*, not their *experience*. Any fool can have an experience and call that his "new birth," but it takes a real Christian to *obey*. That's why Christ

---

[1] I recently spoke about these issues with some ex-Reformed Baptist friends of mine (thus they are ex-Baptist). They spoke of an 8-year-old child from their Reformed Baptist church, who told the mother of this family that "they wouldn't let me get baptized last year, but I've been working really hard so I can get baptized this year." This is sad proof that the Credobaptist church teaches their children to work their way into the kingdom of God, their protestations to the contrary notwithstanding.

gave us obedience as our guideline. But it's so much easier to just trust in some experience, isn't it? That's why I think the Baptistic line of thinking is so popular. It doesn't matter if your children are obedient; as long as they have been "born again," they are safe in God's hands. People take comfort in the "decisions" that their children make, while they show no real fruit. They say with much passion, "But I know his heart is right! He has given his life to Christ!" They take comfort in this instead of taking comfort in their obedience, as the Apostle asserts, "I have no greater joy than to hear that my children *walk* in truth" (3 John 4). Obedience is universally held up as the proof of being a Christian; and contrary to today's American culture, children are obedient to their parents when they have been raised "in the training and admonition of the Lord." It's amazing that there are parents who actually bank on their children's "conversion" as a means to obedience, instead of training.

If you are a Christian, your children belong to God. God has claimed them for Himself, and bids you to "bring them up in the training and admonition of the Lord" (Eph. 6:4).

God's Sign or Yours?

It has been said that baptism is an outward sign of inward grace. I don't necessarily disagree with that assessment; but I must ask, "To whom does the sign belong?" Is it *my* sign, or *God's* sign? Is baptism my declaration to the world that I have now cast off my paganism, and am now committing my life to Christ, as the Baptists assert? Or is it God setting His seal upon a people that He has chosen for Himself?

This is one of the parallels between Old Testament circumcision and New Testament baptism which Paedobaptists are so fond of pointing out. Was circumcision a declaration to the world that someone was a Jew? Obviously not; since nobody ever knew that you were circumcised, except for you, your parents, the man who circumcised you, your wife, those whom you tell, and God. Their *life of obedience* to God's law was their declaration to the world that they were Jews, not their circumcision. Keeping the Sabbath, wearing tassels on the corners of their garments, not eating pork, and following all the rest of God's commands—that was what the world saw, and that was what made them say, "There goes a Hebrew." Circumcision, on the other hand, was God's seal upon them; it was like a stamp of ownership. It was something which an Israelite could remember, and say with much comfort, "The Lord has His mark upon me."

Is baptism the same? Well, who knows that you're baptized? You, the man who baptized you, your parents, your wife, those that you tell, and God. It's the same thing. Nobody looks at you and says, "Hey, there goes a Christian because I can see that he has been baptized!" On the contrary, people look upon our *lives of obedience* to God as the sign that we belong to Him, just like they did with the Jews. The world sees us going to church and worshipping God; they see us loving one another; they see us abstaining from their sinful lifestyle; they see us dressing differently, and talking differently; what they see is what makes us stand out as Christians. So if our baptism is not our "declaration to the world" that we belong to Christ, then what is it? Just like circumcision, it is God's seal of ownership. On the inside cover of each of my books, I put a stamp that proves it belongs to me. God does the same thing with those who belong to Him.

THE SELF-WASHINGS

The Credobaptists whom I have dealt with are fond of pointing to the various self-washings of the Old Testament as proof for the mode of immersion. Of course, it takes quite a leap to get there, because they were not *administered* washings, and Christian baptism *is* an *administered* washing. But they *must* get there because they have nothing else. So let's take a moment to address these washings.

First, we can point out that the Old Testament self-washings were never called *purifications*. But John 3 confirms that Christian baptism *is* a *purification*. And of course, the only purifications in the Bible are administered by sprinkling.

Secondly, the self-washings, being *self*-administered, represented nothing but our own self-assertions in our sanctification. That is how the inspired Apostles viewed them...

> Therefore, having these promises, beloved, let us cleanse ourselves from all filthiness of the flesh and spirit, perfecting holiness in the fear of God (2 Cor. 7:1).

> Cleanse your hands, you sinners; and purify your hearts, you double-minded (James 4:8).

The Apostles would never say something like that regarding your baptism, because baptism is not *your* work. It's a sign of the work of the Spirit. This is why you have *someone else* do the baptizing. Self-washings represent *our* work in sanctification.

Also, please notice that while there are many times in the Old Testament when persons are commanded to "wash" themselves, and sometimes even to wash their entire bodies, this in no way implies *immersion*. I hate to point out the obvious; but unfortunately, I must. These people were in a desert. They didn't carry bathtubs to fill up at the local brook. The water they carried was precious. It was the source of physical life. They did not waste it. And it only takes a rudimentary knowledge of the Old Testament to know that they often came close to perishing for lack of water. As the people of Israel travelled the wilderness, God had to miraculously make water spring from rocks in order to keep them alive. And yet all that time, these people were under the mandates to "wash" themselves. How did they do it? I assure you, it wasn't by immersion.

I like to ask my Credobaptist brethren how many of them "bathed" today. They all answer in the affirmative, of course; and then I ask them how many did it by immersion. (*Cue the cricket noises.*) You see, even in modern America, we don't *bathe* by immersion. We have an abundance of water, and yet we take showers. It's quicker and easier, and it wastes less water. Do you think we are more cognizant of saving water than those who dwelt in the wilderness of Sinai? Today's average bathtub holds 50 gallons of water. And even in one of these, a grown man can hardly immerse his entire body in it. I know I cannot. My knees would stick out if I put my head under (which I never do, of course). Most people who take baths in bathtubs do not immerse, either. They usually soak, and then get up and turn the shower on to wash off the dirty, soapy water. Even if the Credobaptist's immersion position was remotely possible, the amount of water necessary to do the ritual self-cleansings would be too much to comprehend.

To drive this point home, let's ask ourselves some very basic questions.

First, how many of you would like to be the second person in a 50-gallon bathtub today? Sounds yummy, huh? Well, what if you went right after Bildad? Bildad has had a hard day's work out in the fields, and he has just drawn 50 gallons of water from the well, a quarter mile away, to fill up the bathtub.[1] Now, Bildad takes his bath; and then you have to "bathe in water," due to ritual uncleanness. Are

---

[1] Many people forget that they still had to draw water from wells. Of course, they would not defile their wells by bathing in them. Look at these references.

"Behold, **here I stand by the well of water**, and the daughters of the men of the city are coming out **to draw water**. (Gen 24:13, 14).

"Moses fled from the face of Pharaoh and dwelt in the land of Midian; and he sat down **by a well**. Now the priest of Midian had seven daughters. **And they came and drew water,** and they filled the troughs to water their father's flock. Then the shepherds came and drove them away; but Moses stood up and helped them, and watered their flock. When they came to Reuel their father, he said, "How is it that you have come so soon today?" And they said, "An Egyptian delivered us from the hand of the shepherds, and **he also drew enough water for us** and watered the flock" (Ex. 2:15-19).

As they went up the hill to the city, **they met some young women going out to draw water,** and said to them, "Is the seer here?" (1 Sam. 9:11)

Even in the days of Christ, people were still drawing water from wells.

A woman of Samaria came to draw water. Jesus said to her, "Give Me a drink" (John 4:7).

you going to draw 50 more gallons; or will you go ahead and take a bath in the nasty, defiled water that Bildad just left? These people didn't have running water. They had to get it from wells or rivers. And how many bathtubs do you suppose they had to carry around in the wilderness?

Second, how often do you think these people had to bathe? Once a month or so? Only when they came to a river? That's what some people actually think about those desert wanderers. But the Bible tells us differently.

How many people were in Israel at any given time during the wilderness wanderings? Adam Clarke estimated that 3,263,000 people were in the "Church in the wilderness." Albert Barnes estimated more than 2,000,000. Many others suggest between 2 and 3 million. I was unable to find anyone who suggested a number less than 2,000,000. Out of all those people, we know that there were at least 600,000 men of war (not including the Levite men). Not many men of that age remained unmarried back then. But let's assume 500,000 married couples, just for giggles. With that in mind, let's do some figures. Let's take just one text, and use it to test this theory of immersions in the desert.

> **If any man has an emission of semen, then he shall wash all his body in water,** and be unclean until evening…Also, **when a woman lies with a man, and there is an emission of semen, they shall bathe in water,** and be unclean until evening (Lev. 15:16-18).

Now, I shouldn't have to lead anybody by the hand in order to understand exactly how many times people were required by the law to "bathe in water," just from this *one* text. Knowing the nature of man, I would estimate that a minimum of half a million persons *a day* were required to "bathe in water," from this requirement *alone*. In the Baptist world, that equates to 25 million gallons of water per day, just for bathing—not to mention drinking water. And of course, they would also need to tote 250,000 bathtubs around the desert.[1]

These figures don't even take into account the other circumstances in which the people were required to do a self-washing.[2] So my estimate of how much water was necessary is actually really low. This doesn't even take into account those who wanted to wash simply because they got dirty.

So what's the point of all this? Well, these texts prove that it was *impossible* for the Israelites to wash themselves by immersion. Just like you, they washed with water; but they did it by pouring it over

---

[1] Please also take note that "bathtubs" as we know them were not known at that time. If they submersed themselves at all it was in a lake or river. It would have been impossible for a people on the move to construct wooden barrels sized appropriately for human submersion. And permanent baths such as the Roman type, while equally impossible for the traveling Israelites to use, were not known until shortly before the time of Christ.

[2] **If a woman has a discharge,** and the discharge from her body is blood...**Whoever touches her bed shall** wash his clothes and **bathe in water,** and be unclean until evening. And **whoever touches anything that she sat on shall** wash his clothes and **bathe in water,** and be unclean until evening...**Whoever touches those things shall be unclean; he shall** wash his clothes and **bathe in water,** and be unclean until evening (Lev. 15:19-27). "Speak to the children of Israel, and say to them: **'When any man has a discharge from his body...whoever touches his bed shall** wash his clothes and **bathe in water,** and be unclean until evening. **He who sits on anything on which he who has the discharge sat** shall wash his clothes and **bathe in water,** and be unclean until evening. And **he who touches the body of him who has the discharge shall** wash his clothes and **bathe in water,** and be unclean until evening. **If he who has the discharge spits on him who is clean, then he shall** wash his clothes and **bathe in water,** and be unclean until evening...**He who carries any of those things shall** wash his clothes and **bathe in water,** and be unclean until evening. And **whomever the one who has the discharge touches, and has not rinsed his hands in water, he shall** wash his clothes and **bathe in water,** and be unclean until evening...And **when he who has a discharge is cleansed of his discharge, then he shall** count for himself seven days for his cleansing, wash his clothes, and **bathe his body in running water;** then he shall be clean'" (Lev. 15:2-13). Also see Leviticus 16:3, 4, 23, 24, 26-28; 17:15, 16; 22:4-6; Numbers 19:19; Deuteronomy 23:11.

their bodies. They probably needed a gallon or two per person—*if that*. To assume an immersion bath for each of these washings, is to give up common sense in order to defend an indefensible position.

One writer once stated, "There is nothing to show that one immersion of the whole body was ever required." To this, the famous Credobaptist Alexander Carson replied, "If bathing was required, does not this imply immersion?"[1] And of course, that answer is a resounding *NO*. And what's amazing is that everyone *knows* that bathing does not imply immersion, and yet they will *still* stand by their indefensible position.

As I've pointed out in another section of this book, there were some washings or *purifications* that had to be done by another person. These purifications were always done by an administrator. The administrator represents God, Who truly cleanses us. And the self-washings represent our own efforts in sanctification. John 11:55 tells us that many people went "up to Jerusalem" to "purify themselves." They could wash themselves at home, but this was an administered purification; so they needed to go to Jerusalem in order for someone else to do the purification.

So how do the Baptists view baptism? Is it a self-washing, or an administered purification? Perhaps it's both. That's what it seems to be in Credobaptist baptism. Credobaptists insist that baptism must be the immersion of the entire body, and that a baptizer (administrator) must do the immersing; but as I pointed out in my introduction, this would necessitate that they baptize infants or small children *only*. You see, to all appearances, you would think that Credobaptists had a shared administration of baptism—you do part of it, and the baptizer/administrator does the other part. But if baptism is the entire immersion of the body, then the *baptizer* needs to entirely immerse another person's entire body. He could easily do this to a child. But you see, an adult man immerses *himself* up to his waist, at least. Or do you not count the lower half of his body as part of the immersion? So the baptized person performs, at the very least, half of the immersion; and so he himself is a baptizer. The

---

[1] Alexander Carson. Baptism, Its Mode and Subjects. Pg 326

baptizer is really only there to finish the job that the baptized person started. Do you see the conundrum? With effusion, the entire baptism is done *in its entirety* by the administrator of that baptism. The baptized person has no role in the administration of the baptism.

Of course, I guess it could be argued that baptism is only the immersion of the upper half of the body; and so the baptized person is not performing half of his own baptism because he only goes into the water up to his waist, and the actual baptism is from the waist up. But if this was the case, could a child be baptized by being picked up by his feet and dipped in a river like Achilles? Would that be an acceptable baptism? I don't think Baptists would like that.

You see, if baptism is the entire immersion of the *entire* body, and the baptizer is to complete the *entire* baptism; then only infants and small children *could* be baptized by immersion, unless the baptizer was exceptionally strong—then maybe he could pick up a full-grown adult and dip him. It's a funny thought, but at least it's a consistent one.

Let me conclude this section by simply reinforcing this fact. *Even if it could be proved* that the Israelites carried the appropriate number of tubs around the desert, and even if they faithfully filled them with the amount of water needed every day for total immersions of the thousands of persons who needed them; it would still prove *nothing* in regard to Christian baptism. We do not baptize *ourselves* like they did in these self-washings. Baptism is specifically done by an *administrator,* in order to show that Jesus is the great Baptizer. He baptizes us; we don't baptize ourselves.

THE LAVER

You shall also make a laver of bronze, with its base also of bronze, **for washing.** You shall put it between the tabernacle of meeting and the altar. And you shall put water in it, for **Aaron and his sons shall wash their hands and their feet in water from it.** When they go into the tabernacle of meeting, or when they come near the altar to minister, to burn an offering made by fire to the LORD, **they shall**

wash with water, lest they die. So **they shall wash their hands
and their feet,** lest they die. And it shall be a statute forever to
them—to him and his descendants throughout their generations (Ex.
30:18-21).

Interestingly, if anyone were to look up "laver" in a Bible
encyclopedia, he would find some very different pictures. Some of
them look like a bowl full of water, about waist-high, with priests
putting their hands into it; but others show it to be equipped with
spigots that release the water for them to rinse their hands and feet
under it. The Bible doesn't give any clear indication which way it
was built. But we do know that it was on a stand, so it was up off the
ground. So it was probably not very convenient to wash your feet in
it; unless, of course, it was equipped with spigots, or you took the
water out of the laver and poured it on your feet. It's hard to imagine
otherwise.

So the laver was the source of water for washing at the door of
the tabernacle. And we see that even Aaron and his sons were washed
there.[1] It was the only source of water at "the door of the tabernacle."
So are we supposed to imagine Moses lifting Aaron and his sons,
placing them in a bathtub, and scrubbing them down? Or is it more
probable that Moses took water from the laver, and poured it over
the men? You tell me. But you have no option to say that Aaron
climbed into the laver; because then he himself would have been
doing the washing, as opposed to Moses doing the washing. Moses
was the administrator, so the washing had to be done entirely by
Moses. And after the water was defiled by Aaron, did they change
the water for his sons? If not, would you have liked to go last? The
answer is obvious. Moses did the washing, and he did so by pouring
the water from the laver on the men. No defilement; no need to
change the water; no complications over who is washing whom.

---

[1] "And Aaron and his sons you shall bring to the door of the tabernacle of
meeting, and you shall **wash them with water**" (Ex. 29:4). Also see Exodus
40:12; Leviticus 8:4-6.

But of course, some will be contentious and claim that the priests must have climbed into the laver and immersed themselves therein. This is what the famous Credobaptist commentator and theologian John Gill believed. When explaining how the early Church could have immersed all of their converts in such a short time, he says:

> "What number of private baths were in Jerusalem for ceremonial uncleanness; the many pools in the city, and the various apartments and things in the temple fit for such a use; as the dipping room for the high priest, the molten sea for the common priests, **and the ten brazen lavers, each of which held forty baths of water sufficient for the immersion of the whole body;** all which they might be allowed the use of, as they were of the temple; they *having favor with all the people*."[1]

One would have to give Mr. Gill an *A* for effort; but unfortunately, the laver also contained the water used for washing the animal entrails. The same Hebrew language—*to wash in water*—was used for both the priest and the sacrifice. If immersion was the mode of the priestly washing, then they immersed the innards of the animals in the laver as well. Yuck!

> Then Moses brought Aaron and his sons **and washed them with water**.... And he cut the ram into pieces; and Moses burned the head, the pieces, and the fat. **Then he washed the entrails and the legs in water**. And Moses burned the whole ram on the altar (Lev. 8:6, 20, 21; see also Lev. 1:12, 13; 9:14).

---

[1] John Gill, Body of Divinity pg 913.

The Greatest Self-washing: Namaan

Now we enter into the Credobaptist's one defense from the Old Testament Septuagint in order to support the idea of immersion. Prepare to disappoint your Credobaptist brother again.

Namaan, a leper, came to Israel after hearing of a prophet of Jehovah who could heal the sick. With permission from his king and a letter of recommendation from him, he comes to Israel, seeking this prophet. The narrative is well-known. Namaan shows up at Elisha's doorstep, and Gehazi communicates Elisha's message to Namaan: go and "wash seven times in the Jordan River."

> Now Naaman, commander of the army of the king of Syria, was a great and honorable man in the eyes of his master, because by him the LORD had given victory to Syria. He was also a mighty man of valor, **but a leper**...Then Naaman went with his horses and chariot, and he stood at the door of Elisha's house. And Elisha sent a messenger to him, saying, **"Go and wash in the Jordan seven times, and your flesh shall be restored to you, and you shall be clean."** But Naaman became furious, and went away and said, "Indeed, I said to myself, **'He will surely come out to me, and stand and call on the name of the LORD his God, and wave his hand over the place, and heal the leprosy.'** Are not the Abanah and the Pharpar, the rivers of Damascus, better than all the waters of Israel? Could I not wash in them and be clean?" So he turned and went away in a rage. And his servants came near and spoke to him, and said, "My father, if the prophet had told you to do something great, would you not have done it? How much more then, when he says to you, **'Wash, and be clean'?"** So he went down and dipped seven times in the Jordan, according to the saying of the man of God; and his flesh was restored like the flesh of a little child, and he was clean (2 Kings 5:1-14).

Instantly, we hear a cry from the Baptist camp, yelling, "Dipped! Dipped! He said *dipped!*" And indeed, the Septuagint clearly uses the Greek word "βαπτίζω" to translate the original word in this text.

What is the Paedobaptist to do now? Clearly that word means to *dip,* right? Clearly we have been proven wrong, right? No; not clearly, and not even close to clearly. The word βαπτίζω means to *purify* or *cleanse.* Based upon what we have learned,[1] it would only make sense that the same Jews who referred to the ceremonial purification from the dead as "βαπτίζω," would also use the same word here, *with the same meaning.*[2] Yes, it has the same meaning in this text. How can we say that? It's quite simple, our Credobaptist brethren have erred in that they have not taken into account *the only other leper-cleansing text in the Bible.* Any leper who was to be cleansed needed to be cleansed just like those who were defiled by the dead. And much to the Credobaptist's surprise, we see that they were *sprinkled...*"seven times."

> Then the LORD spoke to Moses, saying, **"This shall be the law of the leper for the day of his cleansing:** He shall be brought to the priest. And the priest shall go out of the camp, and the priest shall examine him; and indeed, if the leprosy is healed in the leper, then the priest shall command to take for him who is to be cleansed two living and clean birds, cedar wood, scarlet, and hyssop. And the priest shall command that one of the birds be killed in an earthen vessel over running water. As for the living bird, he shall take it, the cedar wood and the scarlet and the hyssop, and dip them and the living bird in the blood of the bird that was killed over the running water. **And he shall sprinkle it seven times on him who is to be cleansed from the leprosy, and shall pronounce him clean,** and shall let the living bird loose in the open field. He who is to be cleansed shall wash his clothes, shave off all his hair, and wash himself in water, that he may be clean. After that he shall come into the camp, and shall stay outside his tent seven days. But on the seventh day he shall shave all the hair off his head and his beard and his eyebrows—all his hair he shall shave off. He shall wash his clothes and wash his body in water, and he shall be clean (Lev. 14:1-9).

---

[1] See chapter 3
[2] See the note on Ecclesiasticus 31:25, 26 in Chapter 3.

So do we think it's a coincidence that Elisha, a prophet of Jehovah, would command a leper to *wash* "seven times" to make him
"clean," when the *only time* in the Word of God in which a "cleansing"
is performed "seven times,"[1] happens to be the sprinkling of lepers
who were being cleansed? Either this is a remarkable coincidence,
or else Elisha actually knew the symbolic equivalence of what was
happening.

So, per Elisha's command to "wash seven times," Namaan went
to the Jordan and poured water over the area where the leprosy was.
Remember, he was expecting Elisha to come out and wave his hand
"over the place" and heal the leprosy.[2] Elisha did not command

---

[1] Of course, this does not include the purification of silver, described in Psalm
12:6: "The words of the LORD *are* pure words, *Like* silver tried in a furnace of
earth, Purified seven times." Do you notice how fire is a purifying influence? It's
just like baptism. Could it be that this is what *baptism with fire* is supposed to
represent?

[2] Surprisingly, and somewhat shockingly, some Credobaptists have tried to paint
another picture of Naaman's baptism by partial quotes of Scripture. Look at how
this particular Credobaptist (quoted below) tries to make the leprosy cover the
entire body. Then, shockingly, he connects his baptism to the law in Leviticus that
I have quoted (which says that the leper must be sprinkled seven times), but he
says that Namaan "dipped himself seven times," per the law! I'm not joking. Read
it for yourself. I have no fear of any impartial reader examining the law in Leviticus
to determine who is reading it correctly. This is as clear a case of apparent
intentional misleading, if ever I saw one. Here is the quote:
"By the word 'wash' it is obvious that Elisha meant bathe, or dip: the whole
body being leprous, the whole was to be washed. To dip, also, was a definite act
which could be repeated seven times; but any other washing would be indefinite,
and the leper would not know whether any amount of washing at one time could
be taken for seven washings. Elisha also clearly referred in this command to the
Mosaic law respecting the leper, which was as follows: 'He that is to be cleansed
shall wash his clothes, and shave off all his hair, and wash himself in water, that he
may be clean' (Lev. 14:8). As the leper was wholly unclean, he must be wholly
washed. The command, therefore, meant that he should bathe himself, and so the
Jews correctly understood it...When, therefore, Elisha said, 'Go and wash thyself
in Jordan,' he meant, 'Go and bathe thyself, according to the law of the leper on
the day of his cleansing.' Of course, Naaman, if he fulfilled the command of Elisha,
must necessarily bathe himself in the Jordan seven times; and the narrative
accordingly relates, 'Then went he down and dipped himself in the Jordan seven

Namaan to immerse himself, but only to "wash" himself; and he did so. The translators who wrote the Septuagint understood him to have purified himself in a ceremonial way; so they translated the word as βαπτίζω, just as they used the same term for the purification from the dead in Numbers 19. They did not mean to convey the idea that Namaan submersed his entire body in the Jordan. Every cleansing or purification in the Bible comes down from above. Going under the water is representative of death and judgment in the Bible. (Example: the Flood.)

Namaan was an unclean Syrian Gentile. He was not to partake of the sacrifices that were offered by God's people on the altar at the temple. However, Elisha still pointed out to this Gentile that he needed to "wash" seven times. This is remarkable. Even our Lord, when He referred to this story in the Gospel of Luke, referred to it as a "cleansing" or "purification"—the same word used in John 3:25, referring to baptism. And according to our Lord's own exposition of this passage (Luke 4:27), Namaan's cleansing had direct reference to the future acceptance of the Gentiles into the Church. So it's quite clear that Elisha commanded the cleansing without the sacrifice, in order to foreshadow the future inclusion of Gentiles into the Church.

BAPTIZED BY WASHING HANDS

In another blow to the Credobaptist theory of baptism, we see that persons were considered "baptized" when they only washed *their hands*. Please notice carefully that the text does not say that *their hands* were baptized; instead, it says that *they*—that is, *the persons*—were baptized.

> And as He spoke, a certain Pharisee asked Him to dine with him. So He went in and sat down to eat. **When the Pharisee saw it, he**

---

times.'" David Ford, Studies on Baptism pg 230 quoting from Ingham's Handbook on Baptism p. 292.

marveled that He had not first washed [baptized; ἐβαπτίσθη] before dinner (Luke 11:37, 38).

Now, after reading that, most reasonable persons would acknowledge that the Pharisees did not immerse themselves prior to eating. I think that most Credobaptists are reasonable people who will see this quite clearly when they are shown. However, the defenders of the Credobaptist theory are by no means always reasonable. They will defend to the death the idea that they immersed themselves prior to their meals, and that they even immersed their couches (Mark 7:4); they must do so in order to defend their theory.[1] More than likely, you will never meet one of these defenders; for your average Credobaptist, it's pretty easy to show them common-sense stuff. Just point out the other texts that talk about what the Pharisees did before eating...

For the Pharisees and **all the Jews do not eat unless they wash their hands** in a special way, holding the tradition of the elders (Mark 7:3).

Why do Your disciples transgress the tradition of the elders? For **they do not wash their hands when they eat** bread (Matt. 15:2).

You see, the Pharisees were used to washing their hands prior to meals, much like we do today. But to them, it was more than just cleanliness; it was symbolic purification. And of course, according to Luke 11:38, it was referred to as *baptism*. Now we only need to point out that in the same way that someone would come and wash a person's feet, they would also pour the water for the washing of hands. And if you had no servant who could pour it for you, you would simply pour with one hand and then the other. You would either use a pitcher or a ladle.

But Jehoshaphat said, Is there not here a prophet of the LORD, that we may enquire of the LORD by him? And one of the king of Israel's

---

[1] See the quote from Alexander Carson in Chapter 2 section "The Word".

servants answered and said, **Here is Elisha** the son of Shaphat, **which poured water on the hands of Elijah** (2 Kings 3:11).

So the pouring out of water on someone's hands was said to be a *baptism* of the person. Do you see a common theme? It's always effusion, and it does not matter how much of the person gets wet; the person is still *baptized*.

Chapter 7

Answering Credobaptist Objections

Prepositions

Although this topic is in a later chapter of this book, sometimes it might be a good idea to discuss the issue of prepositions right up front with your Credobaptist brother. These little words have been of great use to both sides of the argument, and they have also been a thorn in the side to both sides of the argument.

Let me explain the issue. Greek prepositions are notorious for having many different meanings that are supposed to be determined from context. It doesn't take a genius to figure out that this can lead to some pretty stiff debate. For instance...the Greek preposition ἐν can mean the following:

"in, at, (up-) on, by, etc.: - about, after, against, almost, altogether, among, as, at, before, between, (here-) by (+ all means), for (. . . sake of), give self wholly to, (here-) in (-to, -wardly), mightily, (because) of, (up-) on, [open-] ly, X outwardly, one, quickly, shortly, speedily, that, there (-in, -on), through (-out), (un-) to(-ward), under, when, where (-with), while, with (-in). Often used in compounds, with substantially the same import; rarely with verbs of motion, and then not to indicate direction, except (elliptically) by a separate (and different) prep."[1]

The Bauer lexicon states, "The uses of this preposition are so many-sided, and often so easily confused, that a strictly systematic treatment **is impossible.**" Then it goes on to give four pages of detailed categories of meaning.

Lastly, we have Thayer's very simple definition:

1) in, by, with *etc.*

So when a verse says, "I indeed baptize you *with* (ἐν) water unto repentance, but He who is coming after me is mightier than I, whose sandals I am not worthy to carry. He will baptize you *with* (ἐν) the Holy Spirit and fire" (Matt. 3:11); are we to understand this to mean "in water" or "with water"? It makes a pretty big difference, doesn't it? Go one way, you're a Credobaptist; go the other way, you're a Paedobaptist.

After having studied this issue to an extreme, I think the best way to approach this with a Credobaptist is to just diffuse it right up front and say, "We can't know." It's very difficult to *prove* one way or the other. Of course, you can appeal to context and the other ways in which the word is used in other Scriptures. But it can still be said that it *could* mean the opposite. For instance, John the Baptizer could have said that he baptized *"in* water." You can then show that this would necessitate that we must be baptized *"in* the Holy Spirit." And you could also show that this preposition is used to refer to anointing as well. So Aaron was anointed *"in* oil," etc. And you know what your friend will say? "But it still *could* mean *'in.'"* We are at an impasse; and I think it's best to set the tone right up front: this debate is going to be won or lost *without* the help of prepositions.

Lewis Sperry Chafer is a famous dispensationalist who is no friend to Covenant Theology; and yet he has a great little article in which he quite fairly represents both sides of the argument between

---

[1] Strong's Concordance

Credobaptism and Paedobaptism. A section of that article deals with the prepositions that are so often invoked in order to sway this debate one way or the other. I have inserted that section here.

> "The Prepositions Employed. The usual impression regarding the mode of ritual baptism which one might gain who reads only the English text of the New Testament is molded more by the prepositions that are used in the English text than by any other factor in the case. Four prepositions come up at once for consideration. The point to be developed which concerns all of serious mind is that the particular translation of these prepositions as found in the English text is not the only meaning which the same English text assigns to these words in other like instances. All familiar with the Greek text recognize that a great latitude of meaning is given to prepositions, and that usually the correct sense will be determined by the more or less obvious meaning belonging to the text in which the word is found. It should hardly be needful to state that because a certain translation appears in the English text it is not necessarily the best rendering. The prepositions to be considered are:
>
> ἐν, which has 36 possible meanings and which in Matthew 3:6 has been translated 'in Jordan' is also translated in the English Bible by the words *at, on,* or *with* 330 times, could be so translated in the text cited. The sense is somewhat changed when it is translated 'at Jordan' rather than 'in Jordan.'
>
> ἀπὸ has 20 English meanings, and is used thus in Matthew 3:16: "And Jesus, when he was baptized, went up straightway out of the water." This preposition, here translated *out of,* is translated by the word *from* 374 times in the New Testament and could properly be so translated in Matthew 3:16, in which case the declaration would be that Jesus went up straightway *from* the water.
>
> εἰς has 26 meanings in English and is used in Acts 8:38 for the declaration that "they went down both *into* the water, both Philip and the eunuch; and he baptized him." This preposition is translated in the New Testament 538 times by the word *unto* and could as accurately be so rendered here. It will be observed that going unto or into the water did not constitute the baptism, for Philip also went in with the eunuch.

ἐκ has 24 English meanings and is translated in Acts 8:39 thus, "And when they were come up *out of* the water . . ." This same word is translated *from* 168 times in the New Testament and could as correctly have been so translated here. Thus it would read that Philip and the eunuch went down unto the water and came up from the water.

Though the immersionist depends much on the way these prepositions are translated in order to establish the mode of ritual baptism, **the affusionist contends that the mode of baptism cannot be determined by the prepositions used.**"[1]

Obviously, this argument can be swayed whichever way one wants to see it go. Using these stats from Mr. Chafer should help convince Credobaptists that this is indeed the case. Therefore, I conclude that we should win the debate elsewhere, and then adopt the rendering of the prepositions accordingly.

ORIGINAL LANGUAGES

One day, I was in a discussion with a dear Credobaptist friend, and the conversation was not going well for him. I brought up a particular passage of Scripture (Matthew 28), which tells us to "make disciples of all nations." My friend responded, "That's not what it says; it says to *teach* the nations." Of course, my friend was quoting from the King James Version. I don't mind the KJV; but when I pointed out that the Greek text uses the word μαθητεύσατε (which means to make *disciples* or *learners*), he did not accept that, because I had to use the Greek. Well, we must try to help such persons understand that even the translators *could* have been wrong. If you run into someone like this, I have a helpful illustration that may clear things up for him. Read Luke 14:10 in the King James Version:

---

[1] Systematic Theology volume 7, pgs 39-40.

> But when thou art bidden, go and sit down in the lowest room; that
> when he that bade thee cometh, he may say unto thee, Friend, go up
> higher: *then shalt thou have worship* in the presence of them that sit at
> meat with thee.

Then point out to your brother that men are not to receive
worship. Of course, he will agree with you; and then you can point
out that the Greek word used in that passage is δόξα,[1] meaning
"glory." Tell him that it should be translated *glory,* just as it is translated everywhere else in the KJV. That does not challenge anything
that he doesn't already believe. And once he agrees to your propo-
sition, you can then point out his bias. The reason why he was very
willing to accept the *glory* situation, was because it did not involve a
pet theology. Then bring Matthew 28 into the equation, and he will
balk. You have just shown him his bias, based purely upon his pre-
conceived ideas.

The original languages are important. We can't settle a debate
that has haunted the Church for hundreds of years, unless we are
willing to acknowledge that the translators of our Bibles *may* have
gotten it wrong. I say *"may,"* because I believe that the default
position is to assume that they did translate it correctly. But we have
to be careful, because everyone—including Bible translators—have
their own biases. And unfortunately, those biases (or just plain
mistakes) sometimes make it into a translation.

THE MEDIATOR "PROBLEM"

A popular argument has been coming from the Reformed
Credobaptist camp recently. It deals with the nature of Christ's role
as Mediator of the New Covenant, and how that applies to non-
believers. The argument is usually stated in a "gotcha" question, like
this...

---

[1] We get "doxology" from this word.

"If Christ is the Mediator of the New Covenant, and He mediates only for believers in the New Covenant; then how can He mediate for an unbelieving infant?"

...or something to that effect. The Credobaptists use this argument so consistently that I believe they think they have stumbled upon the Achilles' heel of the Paedobaptist position, and they are exploiting it for all it's worth. But once again, I must differ with their conclusions. It is interesting to note that it only took a brief perusal of the Credobaptist writers themselves to verify that they actually agree with all Paedobaptist theologians on the answer to their own conundrum.

Is Christ the Mediator for all persons in the New Covenant? Of course He is. All—*without exception*. So how can He mediate for an infant that doesn't believe? Oh my, what a problem they have created, huh? Don't gloat as you instruct them in their own theology. Christ is Mediator in more ways than one. By "Mediator," my Credo brethren wrongly deduce that He is the *advocate* of all whom He is *mediating* for. This is an error of no small import. As you can verify from any good Baptist Systematic Theology,[1] as well as their own 1689 Baptist Confession,[2] Christ is the Mediator of the New Covenant *as* Prophet, Priest, *and King*. He advocates for us by pleading His priestly blood on behalf of His elect, and He brings down all the curses of the covenant upon those who reject Him as King of the Covenant.

---

[1] For example, John Gill's Body of Divinity, pg 424 say's "His office in general is that of **Mediator**, which is but one; **the branches of it are threefold, his prophetic, priestly, and kingly offices**".

[2] "It pleased God, in His eternal purpose, to choose and ordain the Lord Jesus, His only begotten Son, according to the covenant made between them both, **to be the mediator between God and man; the prophet, priest, and king**; head and savior of the church, the heir of all things, and judge of the world; unto whom He did from all eternity give a people to be His seed and to be by Him in time redeemed, called, justified, sanctified, and glorified." London Baptist Confession of Faith of 1689, Chapter 8, Of Christ The Mediator, Paragraph 1. Emphasis mine.

Perhaps an example will help illustrate how Christ can be Mediator in these three ways. Was Moses the mediator of the Mosaic covenant? Did he advocate for his people? Of course he did; check out Exodus 32:11-13, where he intercedes for the people of God in a Christ-like fashion, and pleads for their forgiveness. Then he proceeds to go down the mountain and bring judgment upon the wicked (Ex. 32:15-28). He was the mediator as both priest *and King*.

So how does Christ mediate for an unbelieving infant? Well, if the infant's name is written in the Book of Life, then Christ advocates for him before the Father, and pleads His High-Priestly blood. If the infant is numbered among the reprobate, then Christ judges him as his King. It's that easy. But after all, it's not for us to know. Baptist theology has us dwelling on the unknowable in order to perhaps come up with a way to prove their assertions. And once again, they have fallen flat.

UNBREAKABLE?

In keeping with this idea of the Mediator "problem," Credobaptists will also try to say that the New Covenant is "unbreakable." They are trying to make the case that only regenerate persons are included in the New Covenant. When it's pointed out to them that they have unregenerate baptized persons in their churches, they simply reply that "they are not *truly* in the Covenant."

Of course, this is an unprovable position, dwelling on yet another unknowable question. No one sees "elect" stamped on anyone's forehead. So no one can know for sure who the eternally elect are. We are only given outward evidence of who are in the Church, but we have no such evidence of who are eternally elect. We can never go beyond that, and we shouldn't try to, since the "secret things belong to the Lord our God." Leave election in God's hands, and concentrate on what the Lord *has* given you to know and understand.

So why has this line of attack become popular? Because Credobaptists are trying to rule out a Paedobaptist using the idea of the *covenant breaker*. Paedobaptists point to covenant-breakers as proof that unregenerate persons are counted as covenant members throughout the Bible. Credobaptists can't have that in their *"regenerate-only* club"; so they have come up with the "unbreakable covenant" idea, in order to deny the fact that covenant-breakers can exist in the New Covenant. In my view, after having read much on this supposed argument, I think it's an issue of theological maturity. The Credobaptist position has simply not matured enough for them to accept the plain fact that they can't know who the elect are, and that the "Church" that Jesus founded consists of both elect and non-elect. They have not formulated their doctrine of election to take into account the entirety of Scripture.

In the Old Testament, election primarily had the meaning of being "chosen unto great privileges," not "unto eternal life." Therefore, we should expect the same interpretation of election to be taught in the doctrine of Paul. I am a Calvinist through and through, but I also recognize that ALL of the Old Testament people of God were called "elect." And many of the Old Testament "elect" went to hell. I also fully admit that if anyone gets to heaven, it's because of God's sovereign ordination, and not our own efforts. But I have a mature enough theology to recognize that the New Testament has the same theological paradigm. There is an "elect" people chosen unto wonderful privileges, many of whom will go *to hell* because they spurn those privileges; and there are those who are ordained by God unto eternal life, and they are also sometimes referred to as "elect." This is such an obvious conclusion that it seems silly for me to try to prove it. But I know I must, so here it goes...

For you are a holy people to the LORD your God; the LORD your God **has chosen you** to be a people for Himself, a special treasure above all the peoples on the face of the earth. The LORD did not set His love on you nor **choose you** because you were more in number than any other people, for you were the least of all peoples (Deut. 7:6, 7).

The LORD delighted only in your fathers, to love them; and **He chose their descendants after them**, you above all peoples, as it is this day (Deut. 10:15).

"But you, Israel, are My servant, Jacob **whom I have chosen**, The descendants of Abraham My friend (Isa. 41:8).

For Jacob My servant's sake, And Israel **My elect**, I have even called you by your name; I have named you, though you have not known Me (Isa. 45:4).

Now, it should be quite clear to everyone that when the term "chosen" and "elect" are used by God about the nation of Israel, it certainly does not mean that the entire nation was "chosen" or "elect" *unto eternal life*, but rather unto the privileges of being *His special people*. Some—indeed, many—of His people apostatized and went to an eternal punishment. Well, in the New Testament, it's the same way. The term "elect" does not *always* carry the meaning of "chosen unto eternal life." The Apostles used it many times in the same sense as they were used to it being used in the Old Testament. Notice how Peter uses it here:

Peter, an apostle of Jesus Christ, To the pilgrims of the Dispersion in Pontus, Galatia, Cappadocia, Asia, and Bithynia, **elect** according to the foreknowledge of God the Father, in sanctification of the Spirit, for obedience and sprinkling of the blood of Jesus Christ: Grace to you and peace be multiplied (1 Peter 1:1, 2).

But **you are a chosen generation**, a royal priesthood, a holy nation, His own special people, that you may proclaim the praises of Him who called you out of darkness into His marvelous light (1 Peter 2:9).

Did Peter infallibly know that everyone he was writing to was eternally chosen unto salvation? Did Paul know that?

Therefore, **as the elect of God**, holy and beloved, put on tender mercies, kindness, humility, meekness, longsuffering (Col. 3:12).

Obviously, the Apostles did not have infallible knowledge of who were chosen "unto salvation," because they baptized Ananias and Sapphira, as well as many others who were apostates. But they still used the "chosen/elect" language because that's exactly what they were used to from their reading of the Old Testament. So when they give warnings to the "elect" whom they were writing to, we should not be surprised by it; rather, we should expect those words to be used by the Apostles with the same meaning as their Bibles used it. This only makes sense. But this is not to say that there is not an election of grace, by which persons are saved, and without which nobody will be saved. On the contrary, I acknowledge that persons are "appointed to eternal life," as it says in Acts 13:48. This point just acknowledges that the word *elect* is used in different ways at different times, and we need to view the context in order to see what it is actually teaching; and it doesn't always fit with our systematic theological constructs.

So with this in mind, notice how the New Testament authors give warnings to those *in the church,* not to apostatize.

For false christs and false prophets will rise and show great signs and wonders to deceive, if possible, ***even the elect*** (Matt. 24:24).

Of how much worse punishment, do you suppose, will he be thought worthy who has trampled the Son of God underfoot, counted the blood of the covenant **by which he was sanctified** a common thing, and insulted the Spirit of grace? (Heb. 10:29)

For *it is* impossible for ***those who were once enlightened***, and ***have tasted the heavenly gift***, and ***have become partakers of the Holy Spirit***, and ***have tasted the good word of God*** and the powers of the age to come, if they fall away, to renew them again to repentance, since they crucify again for themselves the Son of God, and put *Him* to an open shame (Heb. 6:4-6).

Every branch *in Me* that does not bear fruit He takes away; and every *branch* that bears fruit He prunes, that it may bear more fruit. You are already clean because of the word which I have spoken to you. Abide in Me, and I in you. As the branch cannot bear fruit of itself, unless it abides in the vine, neither can you, *unless you abide in Me*. "I am the vine, you *are* the branches. He who abides in Me, and I in him, bears much fruit; for without Me you can do nothing. If anyone does not abide in Me, he is cast out as a branch and is withered; and they gather them and throw *them* into the fire, and they are burned (John 15:2-6).

You have become estranged from Christ, you who *attempt to* be justified by law; *you have fallen from grace* (Gal. 5:4).

And you, who once were alienated and enemies in your mind by wicked works, yet now He has reconciled in the body of His flesh through death, to present you holy, and blameless, and above reproach in His sight—*if indeed you continue in the faith*, grounded and steadfast, and are not moved away from the hope of the gospel which you heard, which was preached to every creature under heaven, of which I, Paul, became a minister (Col. 1:21-23).

If members of the Church are warned to not fall away from the faith, then it's quite clear that there can be "covenant-breakers" in the New Covenant. The way by which so-called "Reformed" Baptists get around this clear doctrine, is by shear denial. They will say things like, "Those only *appear* to be warning passages," or, "Those are disputed passages." Well, of course they are disputed; they don't fit the Credobaptist theology, so they must dispute them lest they have to change their theology. I actually heard a Reformed Baptist preach on Colossians 1:23 as if it were a *comfort* passage. He took the "if indeed you continue in the faith"; and instead of warning his flock to be diligent and "continue in the faith," he actually took a clear warning and told his flock that it's not a warning; it's actually an encouragement that "you will continue in the faith" because, of course, they are *the elect*. So in the face of this, how is a Christian supposed to be warned to stay on the right path? Apparently, he's not. He's just told that he *will* stay on the right path *if* he's elect. To say otherwise contradicts their very name of "elect," right? This is simply not taking all of the biblical data into account. All of the warning passages only make sense in anyone's theology if we allow for covenant-breakers.

A PHYSICAL KINGDOM VS. A SPIRITUAL KINGDOM?

One of the more popular arguments that Credobaptists use when challenged about the similarities between the New Testament sacraments and the Old Testament sacraments, is their imagined separation between the Old Testament "physical kingdom" and the New Testament "spiritual kingdom." A good example of this reasoning is described by Sam Renihan in his article "The Case for Credobaptism."

A positive credobaptist argument asserts that the relevant covenant involved is the new covenant, and that this covenant is distinct from the biblical covenants that preceded it in history, particularly the Abrahamic covenant. **Simply put, the Abrahamic covenant promised earthly blessings to an earthly people (Abraham and his offspring) in an earthly land.** This covenantal relationship was expanded and developed in the Mosaic covenant and the Davidic covenant (the Mosaic covenant added laws for life in Canaan, and the Davidic covenant provided kings over the people). These three covenants established and governed the kingdom of Israel, comprised of Abraham's people. **The new covenant (i.e., covenant of grace) promises heavenly blessings to a heaven-bound people.** Thus the new covenant is established on better promises, different promises. The new covenant alone is the covenant of grace, distinct from the Israelite covenants.[1]

---

[1] Emphasis is mine. The Article can be found at the following web address: http://www.alliancenet.org/placefortruth/article/the-case-for-credobaptism.

Were the promises made to Abraham simply promises of physical land and blessings, as our Credobaptist brethren assert? Is there a clear difference between the spiritual kingdom of Christ and the physical kingdom of Israel? Was Abraham only offered a physical land as a promise? Well, our Credobaptist brethren assert this so often that we must take them at their word that they actually believe it. Please note the emphasized sections of the quoted paragraph above. Mr. Renihan says quite clearly that Abraham was promised "earthly land," and that the New Covenant believers are promised "heavenly blessings." I find this very interesting, because he obviously did not get that from the Bible. The inspired Apostles viewed the Old Testament promises to Abraham as primarily SPIRITUAL. Let's take a look...

> **By faith Abraham** obeyed when he was called to go out to the place which he would receive as an inheritance. And he went out, not knowing where he was going. By faith he dwelt in the land of promise as in a foreign country, dwelling in tents with Isaac and Jacob, the heirs with him of the same promise; **for he waited for the city which has foundations, whose builder and maker is God** (Heb. 11:8-10).

> These all died in faith, not having received the promises, **but having seen them afar off were assured of them, embraced them and confessed that they were strangers and pilgrims on the earth.** For those who say such things declare plainly that they seek a homeland. And truly if they had called to mind that country from which they had come out, they would have had opportunity to return. **But now they desire a better, that is, a heavenly country.** Therefore God is not ashamed to be called their God, for He has prepared a city for them (Heb. 11:13-16).

So according to the *inspired* Apostle, Abraham and the other patriarchs interpreted God's promise as primarily *spiritual*. God promised a homeland. And because of this promise, the patriarchs, according to the inspired Apostle, dwelt in the physical "promised land" as a "foreign country"; and they sought a "heavenly country," a "city which has foundations, whose builder and maker is God." The distinction that our Credobaptist brethren try to make is absolutely a product of their own theory, and it is certainly not drawn from the Bible.

Like Mr. Renihan in the quoted paragraph above, our Credobaptist brethren also tell us that Abraham was only promised a *physical* seed, and that the promise made to Abraham was to an "earthly people." But once again, the Bible differs from their theory.

> **Therefore know that only those who are of faith are sons of Abraham.** And the Scripture, foreseeing that God would justify the Gentiles by faith, preached the gospel to Abraham beforehand, saying, **"In you all the nations shall be blessed." So then those who are of faith are blessed with believing Abraham. ... Now to Abraham and his Seed were the promises made. He does not say, "And to seeds," as of many, but as of one, "AND TO YOUR SEED," who is Christ** (Gal. 3:7-16; see also Gal. 4:22-31).

That certainly sounds like Paul was pretty convinced that the promise made to Abraham was to his *spiritual* seed. That would be us—those who are found in Christ Jesus—the *heavenly* people. And somehow, those silly patriarchs still kept all of those children in all of the covenant functions—both blessings and curses. How could they have been so foolish?

All right, so according to the inspired Apostle, the promises made to Abraham were primarily promising a *spiritual* kingdom—a "heavenly country." But is it possible that the blessing of Abraham was purely physical? After all, God gave him lots of riches, right?

> Christ has redeemed us from the curse of the law, having become a curse for us (for it is written, "CURSED IS EVERYONE WHO HANGS ON A TREE"), that **the blessing of Abraham** might come upon the Gentiles in Christ Jesus, that **we might receive the promise of the Spirit through faith** (Gal. 3:13, 14).

Hmmm..."the promise of the Spirit through faith"? That sounds pretty *spiritual*, doesn't it? All right, so once again, the blessing of

Abraham is interpreted by the Apostle as *spiritual;* but surely Abraham thought the physical blessings which the Lord gave him were the pinnacle of blessings, right? After all, those are what Abraham was after, wasn't he?

> After these things the word of the LORD came to Abram in a vision, saying, "Do not be afraid, Abram. **I am your shield, your exceedingly great reward**" (Gen. 15:1).

With this quotation, I will say that it's time to put away this "Abraham = physical and earthly" garbage. Start interpreting the Bible the way the Apostles did. What more do we need than Christ, our All in all? That is exactly what Abraham was promised, and it is precisely what we have been promised as well. We Christians have the greatest privilege, because we have Jesus as our exceedingly great reward! And He told us, "I WILL NEVER LEAVE YOU NOR FORSAKE YOU" (Heb. 13:5). We have Christ! what more could we ever need? God *Himself* belongs to both Abraham and us. That's pretty *spiritual*. As a matter of fact, that is so spiritual that even our Credobaptist brethren will admit it. Read this...

> *and* **thy exceeding great reward**; ... "the Lord would reward him in a way of grace with greater and better things; nay, he himself would be his reward, and which must be a great one, an exceeding great one; as Christ is to his people in his person, offices, and grace, all being theirs, and he all in all to them; all the blessings of grace and glory coming along with him, and he being their portion here and hereafter, to all eternity; for since he is theirs, all are theirs, all things appertaining to life and godliness, and eternal life itself."[1]

Once again, we have a Credobaptist commentator who cannot help supporting the Paedobaptist argument, because he did not realize it at the time he wrote this. I assure you that if he had known that I was going to look at that comment and use it to disprove his Baptistic ideas, he would not have written it like he did. After all, he

---

[1] John Gill's Commentary on this passage.

was a vehement Credobaptist. But when he wrote this comment, he wasn't thinking of how this text would come into the great debate before us, in any way; and because he didn't know, he did exactly what he was supposed to do, and he interpreted the text as applying perfectly to Christians. And what a beautiful picture he gives of the spiritual blessings which we Christians have. Therefore, the blessing that Abraham received was spiritual as well. God Himself was his "reward." I call the possession of God Himself the greatest "spiritual" reward, and I will leave my Credobaptist brethren to argue otherwise if they wish.

Much Water

Another argument that Credobaptists rely on is the argument from "much water." It goes like this. John the Baptizer baptized in places where there was "much water" (John 3:23); therefore, he obviously needed a lot of water in order to perform immersions. Some Credobaptists will proceed to chide Paedobaptists with the idea that if it only takes a little bit of water, why don't they just use a glass of water? Why did the Ethiopian need outside water to be baptized; why didn't Philip just open up a canteen?

Does that make sense to you? Sure it will—until you actually think about it...like an adult. They were in the...you got it...the *desert*. In the desert, it's not a standard practice to pour out your only drinking water on the ground, no matter what ceremony must be performed. Water is precious. Waste it, and you may die. So you only pour out water when there is an abundance of it. This is so obvious, that you can see how Credobaptists did not originate in the Middle East, but rather in modern Europe, with no shortage of water. After all, I've been in the military, and I've been out camping when water is short. I assure you that none will be spared to wash anyone's hands, unless there is an abundance of it around to fill your canteens with. So of course, John the Baptizer and any other baptizer will not be in the habit of pouring out his very life for that which does not save the soul. If baptism was a source of salvation, the Apostles would have poured out every drop, even in the desert; but simply as a picture of the true baptism of the Holy Spirit, they would not do so, unless plenty of water was available.

For crying out loud, wars were fought in the Bible over water wells. Hagar and Ishmael almost perished for lack of it.[1] Because the Israelites lacked water, they murmured time and time again that Moses was trying to kill them. Water was precious stuff. Take good notice of what Dr. Chafer says about this passage.

> "Considering further the Scripture involved, it may be observed that much has been made of the statement in John 3:23 which reads, "And John also was baptizing in AEnon near to Salim, because there was much water there: and they came, and were baptized." When the arresting words *much water* are properly understood as *many springs*— such as would be required for the physical needs of the throngs of people and their beasts—the passage contributes nothing toward a modal ideal for ritual baptism. AEnon is likely to be identified as a sloping hillside with springs of water, but no body of water available.
>
> Thus, again, the affusionist contends that it cannot be proved from the important Scriptures involved that ritual baptism is appointed to be given by immersion."[2]

And of course, he's right. It can't be proven from all of Scripture that immersion is the required mode of baptism.

The Mikveh

Lastly (and sadly), I must address the issue of the mikveh. It's embarrassing; but I have to do it, because you will inevitably run into someone who has a "Jewish friend" who told them about the mikveh. These people like to point to the Jews' modern practice of

---

[1] Genesis 21:14-19.
[2] Lewis Sperry Chafer, Systematic Theology volume 7, pg 39.

immersing themselves in man-made pools for ritual purification. These pools are referred to as *mikveh*. Then they try to equate the submersion into these pools with our Christian baptism. Well, one thing that *can* be said about my brethren who bring this up, is that at least they see the connection between Christian baptism and purification! However, they err greatly by trying to connect Biblical baptism with the modern mikveh, for a couple of reasons. The first reason is that the mikveh didn't exist. That's right; *it didn't exist*. The modern mikveh is a Jewish adoption of the Roman and Greek bathhouses[1] that came about after Israel became a Roman occupied territory. No mikveh is known to exist prior to the first century BC. And we don't really know if they were used for ritual cleansing or not. We do know that medieval Judaism used the mikveh for ritual purification. But they themselves admit that this is not how it was done in Biblical days.

Although water purification is referred to in the Old Testament, in regard to rituals and the Jewish Temple in Jerusalem, with washing, sprinkling, and dipping in water, we do not hear of specific places or installations that people would constantly frequent for the purpose of ritually cleansing their flesh. The term mikveh was used in a very general sense in the Old Testament to refer to a body of water of indeterminate extent (cf. Gen. 1:10; Ex. 7:19), or more specifically to waters gathered from a spring or within a cistern (Lev. 11:36) or waters designated for a large reservoir situated in Jerusalem (Isa. 22:11). None of these places are mentioned as having been used for ritual purification in any way. Hence, the concept of the mikveh as a hewn cave or constructed purification pool attached to one's dwelling or place of work is undoubtedly a later one. A distinction must be made therefore between the purification practices as they are represented in biblical sources, with Jewish water immersion rituals of the Second Temple

---

[1] They start to appear in history after the Jews were conquered by the Romans. This is probably also why some in the early Greek Church immersed; that was simply their concept of bathing. But in ancient Biblical times, it was with very little water, and it was poured over the person.

period, as well as with later customs of mikva'ot prevailing from medieval times and to the present day.[1]

In other words, the modern mikveh is not the same as the Old
Testament purifications. And this is from the Jewish sources. Press
this home to your Credobaptist friend.

The other reason why the mikveh cannot be compared to
Christian baptism (even if it was of that antiquity), is that it is not an
administered rite. It's a *self-washing;* therefore, it doesn't compare
to Christian baptism.[2]

---

[1] https://www.jewishvirtuallibrary.org/mikveh - 6/22/2018.
[2] See the section on Self-washings in Chapter 6.

Chapter 8

THE CASE FROM ANTIQUITY

In this chapter, it is my intention to show you the historical evidence that supports Paedobaptism by effusion. I do not rest my arguments on the early Church alone; but I do believe that when the early Church sources are taken in conjunction with the Biblical data, a very persuasive argument can be made.

The early Church was entirely made up of Jews at one time, having a Hebrew understanding of Scripture; but at the hand of the Apostle Peter, the Gentiles were graciously called into the Church. At that time in history, Greek culture was prominent. Alexander the Great had done his work well; he started the process of Hellenization, or the "Greekifying" of the world. Greek culture was vastly different from Hebrew culture, and it stressed an individualistic mentality that slowly spread into the mainly-Hebrew Christian Church. The Hebrews are still known today for their family orientation (as I hope you know, simply from reading the Scriptures). If you ever meet orthodox Jews, you will be struck by their tight-knit family and community structures. That's the way the early Church was. The Hebrews had no trouble at all understanding the covenantal nature of the Gospel promises and signs. They baptized their infants as covenant members, giving them the sign of God's promise to them, without blinking an eye. We see proof of this in the early Church, well into the second century AD. When Peter stood up on the day of Pentecost, and told the exclusively Hebrew audience that the promise of God was "to you and to your children," those in the audience understood him perfectly, because that was the language they had grown up with. They had heard the promise to Abraham a million times: "I will establish My covenant between Me and you and your descendants after you." Now they heard the same thing coming from the mouth of an Israelite. Peter was a *real* Israelite—one who had accepted the Messiah Who was promised by God. Now the Hebrews in the audience heard that the God of Israel had sent His Messiah, and that He had established His covenant, once again, with "you and your descendants after you." The Hebrews understood this perfectly.

But Greek thinking soon caught up with the Church, as it became prominently Gentile and less Hebrew. They quickly forgot why they baptized infants; and in order to fill this theological void, the concept of baptismal regeneration became the prevailing reason for baptizing infants, within four hundred years. During the third century AD, we start to see some confusion in the Church, as Greek individualistic thought started to rule the day; and then by the fourth century AD, baptismal regeneration was the preferred explanation as to why infants were baptized. The basis for that doctrine was the saying, "There is no salvation outside the Church." Thus, since baptism was the initiatory rite for the Church, "no baptism = no salvation." No wonder that when the fifteenth and sixteenth centuries came around, so many people rejected infant baptism outright. But please notice that what they were rejecting was the Roman/Greek view of baptism, *not* the Hebrew Covenantal view. They were rejecting the Roman Catholics' baptism of any infant that they could get their hands on, not the covenant baptism that I have explained to you in these pages. When you read the Bible the way it was meant to be understood (Covenantal/Hebrew), you will see that you have rejected an aberrant view of baptism, not the Biblical view of baptism. So if you continue to reject infant baptism after reading this, please make sure that you are rejecting the *real* doctrine, and not a false one, like the doctrine that the Greek Church came up with.

WHAT DO THE FATHERS SAY?

The early Church father **Irenaeus** wrote quite a bit against the Gnostics. Here is a passage that he wrote in *Against Heresies*. He is explaining how the Gnostics had misused the number 30 (of Christ's age) to mean what it did not mean. Notice the eloquence...

> "Being thirty years old when He came to be baptized, and then possessing the full age of a Master, He came to Jerusalem, so that He might be properly acknowledged by all as a Master. For He did not seem one thing while He was another, as those affirm who describe Him as being man only in appearance; but what He was, that He also appeared to be. Being a Master, therefore, He also possessed the age of a Master, not despising or evading any condition of humanity, nor setting aside in Himself that law which He had appointed for the human race, but sanctifying every age, by that period corresponding to it which belonged to Himself. **For He came to save all through means of Himself—all, I say, who through Him are born again to God—infants, and children, and boys, and youths, and old men. He therefore passed through every age, becoming an infant for infants, thus sanctifying infants; a child for children, thus sanctifying those who are of this age, being at the same time made to them an example of piety, righteousness, and submission; a youth for youths, becoming an example to youths, and thus sanctifying them for the Lord.** So likewise He was an old man for old men, that He might be a perfect Master for all, not merely as respects the setting forth of the truth, but also as regards age, sanctifying at the same time the aged also, and becoming an example to them likewise. Then, at last, He came on to death itself, that He might be "the first-born from the dead, that in all things He might have the pre-eminence," the Prince of life, existing before all, and going before all."[1]

What a beautiful description of Christ's humanity being our example at any age! Did you notice, however, that Irenaeus

---

[1] Irenaeus, Against Heresies Book 2. Ante-Nicene Fathers volume 1.

explicitly stated that even infants are among those who can be "born again to God," and that Christ has "sanctified them"? Do you agree with him?

Justin Martyr was a man who lived early in the second century AD, and he is the most prolific of the earliest authors whose writings we have. In one of his books, entitled *A Dialog with Trypho,* he records conversations that he had with a Jew named Trypho. It's fascinating reading for anyone interested in what the earliest Christians believed. I've read it in its entirety, and I loved every page of it. Now remember, Justin was talking to a Jew. Notice how Justin connects Old Testament circumcision with New Testament baptism...

> "As, then, circumcision began with Abraham, and the Sabbath and sacrifices and offerings and feasts with Moses, and it has been proved they were enjoined on account of the hardness of your people's heart, so it was necessary, in accordance with the Father's will, that they should have an end in Him who was born of a virgin, of the family of Abraham and tribe of Judah, and of David; in Christ the Son of God, who was proclaimed as about to come to all the world, to be the everlasting law and the everlasting covenant, even as the forementioned prophecies show. And we, who have approached God through Him, have received **not carnal, but spiritual circumcision,** which Enoch and those like him observed. **And we have received it through baptism,** since we were sinners, by God's mercy; and all men may equally obtain it.[1]

In the early third century AD, a man named **Cyprian** was Bishop of Carthage. He called together a council of **66 bishops,** in order to address a letter which he had received from a Christian brother, who had some questions about infant baptism. After this council of 66 bishops met, they unanimously agreed that, *yes*, infants *could* be baptized prior to day 8. Funny, isn't it? The entire Church rightly considered baptism to have replaced circumcision; and some

---

[1] Justin Martyr, Dialog with Trypho Ch. 43. Ante-Nicene Fathers, volume 1.

took that so far, that they thought that we *must* baptize on the eighth day, and not a day sooner or later. But the propriety of infant baptism was never even discussed! Isn't that amazing?[1]

Thankfully, Cyprian and the council of bishops wisely corrected their erring brother. I quote a shortened form of the letter below...

> "Cyprian, and others his colleagues who were present in council, in number sixty-six, to Fidus their brother, greeting. We have read your letter, dearest brother, in which...[another subject]
>
> ...But in respect of the case of the infants, which you say ought not to be baptized within the second or third day after their birth, and that the law of ancient circumcision should be regarded, so that you think that one who is just born should not be baptized and sanctified within the eighth day, we all thought very differently in our council. For in this course which you thought was to be taken, no one agreed; but we all rather judge that the mercy and grace of God is not to be refused to any one born of man...
>
> ...And therefore, dearest brother, this was our opinion in council, that by us no one ought to be hindered from baptism and from the grace of God, who is merciful and kind and loving to all. Which, since it is to be observed and maintained in respect of all, we think is to be even more observed in respect of infants and newly-born persons, who on this very account deserve more from our help and from the divine mercy, that immediately, on the very beginning of their birth, lamenting and weeping, they do nothing else but entreat. We bid you, dearest brother, ever heartily farewell.[2]

Awesome, isn't it? Justin Martyr, Cyprian, and the 66 bishops in council all say precisely the same thing as the Apostle Paul, when he asserted that we are spiritually "circumcised" when we are "buried with Him in baptism." Look at what Paul said...

---

[1] Never in any of the patristic writings, does anyone make a claim that the Apostles did not baptize children.

[2] Cyprian, Epistle 58 To Fidus, on the baptism of infants. Ante-Nicene Fathers volume 5.

In Him you were also circumcised with the circumcision made without hands, by putting off the body of the sins of the flesh, **by the circumcision of Christ, buried with Him in baptism,** in which you also were raised with Him through faith in the working of God, who raised Him from the dead (Col. 2:11, 12).

Even as late as the fourth century AD, when Augustine was having his controversy with the Donatists[1] over re-baptism, and with the Pelagians over original sin[2]; there was not even a whimper about whether or not it was proper to baptize infants in the first place. Both sides assumed that it was proper.

Some Baptists will quote from the Church Fathers in places where they reference adult baptism, as if that contradicts what Paedobaptists believe. For instance, they will quote the *Didache*, which says:

And before baptism, let the one who is to be baptized fast, as well as any others who are able. Also, you must instruct the one who is to be baptized to fast for one or two days beforehand.

This they quote as proof of the Credobaptist position. Let me be very clear: *all* Paedobaptists believe in adult baptism. It does not help the case of the Baptist to show adults being baptized, because *everyone* baptizes adults. What the Baptist must demonstrate is that the early Christians baptized *only* adults. And that cannot be done. On the contrary, the opposite is what is proven. The early Church unanimously believed that infants of believers should be baptized. Even when disputes arose over this issue, no one ever contested the validity of infant baptism itself; nobody ever said, "The Apostles

---

[1] Many Anabaptists and Baptists try to trace their roots back to the Donatists, because the Donatists stood up for re-baptism. But the Donatists themselves baptized infants; and they only re-baptized those who were baptized by heretics, and those who were not thought to be "true" Christians.

[2] See next section for more on this.

never did it that way." Compare the above quote from the Didache to this statement below:

> And before circumcision, let the one who is to be circumcised fast, as well as any others who are able. Also, you must instruct the one who is to be circumcised to fast for one or two days beforehand.

Would anyone read that statement and conclude that circumcision is for adults *only*? You probably wouldn't, because you already understand circumcision to be primarily for infants. But according to Scripture, circumcision is also for adults who convert to Judaism. And so, *in the context of a Biblical understanding of circumcision,* the above statement would obviously be applied to converts and not to the infant recipients of circumcision. However, if someone had an unbiblical understanding of circumcision, they may read that statement and conclude that, indeed, circumcision must be for adults only, because only adults can "fast." Of course, they would be wrong, because of their unbiblical view of circumcision. The early Church understood baptism to be the replacement of circumcision. So when they read the Didache or any New Testament passage that referenced adult baptism, they understood that it was speaking about adult converts, not addressing the infants of believers at all.

In regard to the mode of baptism, the Fathers have also been quoted by both sides of the debate—Baptists quoting them as speaking of immersion, and Paedobaptists quoting them as speaking of sprinkling. I think the answer is to see what they meant by *immersion.* After all, I'll be the first to admit that sometimes they *do* seem to be speaking about immersion. But they never actually say anything about going under the water. They say "go down into the water," or something like that. Of course, our Credobaptist brethren jump all over these texts. But once we understand what they meant by *immersion,* I don't think they are left with any argument. Note the following illustration.

PLATE 1.—THE BAPTISM OF CHRIST.

This representation is the center-piece in the dome of the Baptistery at Ravenna; which building was erected and decorated A. D. 454.

John the Baptizer is standing on the bank, holding an oblong cross in his left hand, and in his right hand a shell from which he pours water on the head of the Savior as He stands in the water up to His loins. Over the head of the Lord is a crown of glory, and the figure of a dove, symbolizing the Holy Spirit. The figure at the right is a mythological representation of the river Jordan. The immersion so often spoken of by the early Greek and Roman Catholic writers, was nothing more than His standing in the water while He was baptized. Every picture in the world of the Lord's baptism that is older than the sixteenth century, represents the Lord as standing in the water (immersion) while John is always represented as standing on the bank pouring the water on His head (Baptism). It is hard to mistranslate this picture.[1]

---

[1] This entire page, picture and text has been taken from "A Short Method with The Dipping Anti-Pedobaptists." By Thomas Gallaher

To *im*merse means to put an object *into* a medium. It doesn't necessarily mean *under* the medium; but it doesn't rule it out either. To *sub*merse definitely means to put the object *under* the medium. So if I had a glass half-full of water, and I put a pencil in the water, I could say that it was immersed; but I could not say that it was submersed. But if the glass was completely full, and I put the pencil completely under the water, I could then use either word—*immersed* or *submersed*—to describe the object. So, if actually going *under* the water was so important to the early Christians, why did they not just use the word that cannot be mistaken? Why not use *submerse?* The answer is because going under the water was never a part of baptism.[1]

The "immersion" that the Fathers spoke about—the "going down into the water," or the "washing"—is nothing more than someone standing in the water while someone else pours water over

---

[1] Interestingly, the Latin Church Fathers did not use the word *submergo* to describe baptism; they used *immergo*. If they thought that going under the water was so important, then they would have used the word *submergo*, or *submerse*. But their baptismal candidates were simply standing in water (*immergo*); and they were being washed, or baptized, from above, via effusion, and upon completion they emerged (*emergo*) from the water. You can emerge from water whether you were *im*mersed or *sub*mersed.

We get our English word *immerse* from the Latin word *immergo*. The early Latin Church knew their own language pretty well, I would assume. A Latin dictionary defines these terms this way: *immergo*: to plunge into; *submergo*: to plunge under. (http://latin-dictionary.net, on immergo and submergo, 6/23/18)

I also stumbled upon an online physics quiz, which asked the following:

Q - *Distinguish between an immersed and a submerged body.*

A - *An immersed body is partially or completely surrounded by water, whereas a submerged body is completely surrounded by fluid.*
(standing in water // diving underwater)
(boat // submarine)
(https://quizlet.com/109111177/physics-ch-13-flash-cards/, 6/23/18)

It's interesting how they compare "standing in water" as opposed to "diving underwater." That is exactly what we are talking about.

them. Notice what the Didache says concerning the mode of baptism:

> And concerning baptism, thus baptize ye: Having first said all these
> things, baptize into the name of the Father, and of the Son, and of the
> Holy Spirit, in living water. But if thou have not living water, baptize
> into other water; and if thou canst not in cold, in warm. But if thou
> have not either, pour out water thrice upon the head into the name of
> Father and Son and Holy Spirit. But before the baptism let the baptizer
> fast, and the baptized, and whatever others can; but thou shalt order
> the baptized to fast one or two days before.[1]

Now first, remember what I said about the prepositions in
Greek.[2] The Didache was written in Greek, and the prepositions
therein are no exception. When it says, "*in* living water," it could just
as easily say, "*with* living water"; and in some translations of the
Didache, it does say that. So don't read too much into that. What
you *can* see here in this quotation, is that even if it should be
understood as meaning "*in* water," it doesn't prove immersion. The
person stood *in* water while being *poured upon*. This quotation is just
stating that if you had no water to stand in, just do the pouring,
because the pouring *is* the baptism.

Thus, we have the Fathers speaking about both immersion and
effusion in their writings. In proof of this, notice how the Church
father Tertullian says that the candidate for baptism is both immersed
and sprinkled:

> Well, but how great is the force of perversity for so shaking the faith
> or entirely preventing its reception, that it impugns it on the very
> principles of which the faith consists! There is absolutely nothing
> which makes men's minds more obdurate than the simplicity of the
> divine works which are visible in the act, when compared with the

---

[1] Didache, or Teaching of the Twelve Apostles. Chap. 7. Ante-Nicene Fathers
volume 7.

[2] See Chapter 7 section on Prepositions.

grandeur which is promised thereto in the effect; so that from the very fact, **that with so great simplicity, without pomp, without any considerable novelty of preparation, finally, without expense, a man is dipped (immersed) in water, and amid the utterance of some few words, is sprinkled, and then rises again, not much (or not at all) the cleaner, the consequent attainment of eternity is esteemed the more incredible.**[1]

Now, if being immersed meant to be completely *covered* by water instead of just *standing* in water, then how can the person be "sprinkled" before he "rises again" out of the water? Just as the pictures from early centuries show, the candidate stood in water (referred to as *immersion*), and was poured upon (referred to as *washing* or *baptism*).

Both Justin Martyr and Tertullian remark how our baptism was imitated by the heathen nations. Both describe baptism as a "washing," being done by "sprinkling." Justin Martyr says this about those who imitate Christian baptism...

And the devils, indeed, having heard **this washing**[2] published by the prophet, instigated those who enter their temples, and are about to approach them with libations and burnt-offerings, **also to sprinkle themselves; and they cause them also to wash themselves entirely**, as they depart [from the sacrifice], before they enter into the shrines in which their images are set.[3]

And Tertullian says basically the same thing about the heathens imitating Christian baptism by "sprinkling."

Well, but the nations, who are strangers to all understanding of spiritual powers, ascribe to their idols the imbuing of waters with the self-same efficacy." (So they do) but they cheat themselves with waters

---

[1] On Baptism — Tertullian. Chapter 2. Ante-Nicene Fathers Volume 3.
[2] The previous chapter was entitled "Christian Baptism," in which Justin Martyr describes baptism as a "washing."
[3] Justin Martyr, First Apology, Chap. LXII. Baptism's Imitation by Demons. Ante-Nicene Fathers volume 2.

184 | Reasoning with Credo Baptists

which are widowed. For washing is the channel through which they are initiated into some sacred rites - of some notorious Isis or Mithras. **The gods themselves likewise they honour by washings.** Moreover, **by carrying water around, and sprinkling it,** they everywhere expiate country-seats, houses, temples, and whole cities: at all events, at the Apollinarian and Eleusinian games **they are baptized;** and they presume that the effect of their doing that is their regeneration and the remission of the penalties due to their perjuries. Among the ancients, again, whoever had defiled himself with murder, was wont to go in quest of purifying waters. Therefore, if the mere nature of water, in that it is the appropriate material for washing away, leads men to flatter themselves with a belief in omens of purification, how much more truly will waters render that service through the authority of God, by whom all their nature has been constituted! If men think that water is endued with a medicinal virtue by religion, what religion is more effectual than that of the living God? **Which fact being acknowledged, we recognise here also the zeal of the devil rivalling the things of God, while we find him, too, practising baptism in his subjects.** What similarity is there? The unclean cleanses! the ruiner sets free! the damned absolves! He will, forsooth, destroy his own work, by washing away the sins which himself inspires![1]

Even earlier than Justin Martyr and Tertullian, we have the Epistle of Barnabas. The writer connects Numbers 19 and baptism in the very same way that I have, in Chapter 3 of this book.

Now what do you suppose this to be a type of, that a command was given to Israel, that men of the greatest wickedness should offer a heifer, and slay and burn it, and, that then boys should take the ashes, and put these into vessels, and bind round a stick purple wool along with hyssop, and that thus the boys should sprinkle the people, one by one, in order that they might be purified from their sins? Consider how He speaks to you with simplicity. The calf is Jesus: the sinful men offering it are those who led Him to the slaughter. But now the men are no longer guilty, are no longer regarded as sinners. **And the boys**

---

[1] Tertullian – On Baptism, Chap. V. - Use Made of Water by the Heathen. Type of the Angel at the Pool of Bethsaida (Bethesda).

that sprinkle are those that have proclaimed to us the remission of sins and purification of heart. To these He gave authority to preach the Gospel, being twelve in number, corresponding to the twelve tribes of Israel. But why are there three boys that sprinkle? To correspond to Abraham, and Isaac, and Jacob, because these were great with God. And why was the wool [placed] upon the wood? Because by wood Jesus holds His kingdom, so that [through the cross] those believing on Him shall live for ever. But why was hyssop joined with the wool? Because in His kingdom the days will be evil and polluted in which we shall be saved, [and] because he who suffers in body is cured through the cleansing efficacy of hyssop. And on this account the things which stand thus are clear to us, but obscure to them because they did not hear the voice of the Lord.[1]

Cyril, the Bishop of Alexandria, lived in the fifth century AD. In his commentary on Isaiah 4:4, he gives his understanding of baptism. He references the baptism for the dead with water mixed with the ashes of a heifer, and he explains the mode of sprinkling. He wrote:

> We have been baptized, not with bare water, nor with the ashes of a heifer,—We are sprinkled [with these] to purify the flesh, alone, as says the blessed Paul,—but with the Holy Spirit, and fire.[2]

Ambrose also connects baptism with sprinkling, when he comments on the 51st Psalm of David.

> "After the white robes were given to you as a sign that you were putting off the covering of sins and putting on the chaste veil of innocence, of which the prophet said, "Purge me with hyssop, and I shall be cleansed; wash me, and I shall be made whiter than snow." For one who is baptized is seen to be purified according

---

[1] Epistle of Barnabas Chapter 8 Chap. VIII. —The Red Heifer a Type of Christ. Ante-Nicene Fathers Volume 1.

[2] Cyril, Commentary on Isaiah 4:4. As quoted by Samuel Baird in "The Great Baptizer" pg 195.

to the law and according to the gospel: according to the law, because Moses sprinkled the blood of the lamb with a bunch of hyssop; according to the gospel, because Christ's garments were white as snow, when in the Gospel he showed forth the glory of his resurrection. One, then, whose guilt is forgiven is made whiter than snow. Thus God said through Isaiah: "Though your sins are as scarlet, I will make them white as snow."[1]

When the debates in the early Church took place about whether or not baptism should be done again in certain cases, Cyprian had a lot to say. He argued that the baptism performed by heretics should not be accepted as valid. Regardless of your agreement or disagreement, look at what he has to say about baptism.

When we were together in council, dearest brethren, we read your letter which you wrote to us concerning those who seem to be baptized by heretics and schismatics, (asking) whether, when they come to the Catholic Church, which is one, they ought to be baptized. On which matter, although you yourselves hold thereupon the truth and certainty of the Catholic rule, yet since you have thought that of our mutual love we ought to be consulted, we put forward our opinion, not as a new one, but we join with you in equal agreement, in an opinion long since decreed by our predecessors, and observed by us, —judging, namely, and holding it for certain that no one can be baptized abroad outside the Church, since there is one baptism appointed in the holy Church. And it is written in the words of the Lord, "They have forsaken me, the fountain of living waters, and hewed them out broken cisterns, which can hold no water." And again, sacred Scripture warns, and says, "Keep thee from the strange water, and drink not from a fountain of strange water." **It is required, then, that the water should first be cleansed and sanctified by the priest, that it may wash away by its baptism the sins of the man who is baptized; because the Lord says by Ezekiel the prophet: "Then will I sprinkle clean water upon you, and ye shall be cleansed from all your filthiness; and from all your idols will I cleanse you: a new heart also will**

---

[1] Ambrose, Bishop of Milan, On the Mysteries 7.34.

I give you, and a new spirit will I put within you" (Ez. 36:25, 26). But how can he cleanse and sanctify the water who is himself unclean, and in whom the Holy Spirit is not? since the Lord says in the book of Numbers, "And whatsoever the unclean person toucheth shall be unclean" (Num. 19:2). Or how can he who baptizes give to another remission of sins who himself, being outside the Church, cannot put away his own sins?[1]

Let me point out what you may have missed. Cyprian called for the water itself to be "cleansed"; and he calls this cleansing of the water, the water's own "baptism." Very interesting—water being *baptized.* Then, of course, he proceeds to say that the reason the water had to be "cleansed" or "baptized," was so that it will be clean when it's *sprinkled* on the person being baptized. He uses Ezekiel 36:25, 26 as proof of this.

DID THE APOSTLES DO IT?

In Tertullian's book on baptism (in which he quite clearly argues against the practice of infant baptism), he explains that he "preferred" that parents postpone the baptism of their children, simply on the basis of the possible imperfection in the child's upbringing. His view was that we should only baptize the children of parents whom we know will not die before they can do a good job raising their children in the ways of the Lord. It's a noble preference, but it is one that is very hard to administer. Regardless of whether or not we agree with him, he definitely assumed that infant baptism was the standard practice of the church; and he argues his point by nothing other than good, old-fashioned pragmatism. For the same pragmatic reasons, he argues that unmarried men ought not to be baptized until they are married, in order to keep them from sexual temptation, of course.

---

[1] The Epistles of Cyprian, Epistle 69. Ante-Nicene Fathers volume 5.

And so, according to the circumstances and disposition, and even age, of each individual, **the delay of baptism is preferable; principally, however, in the case of little children.** For why is it necessary - if (baptism itself) is not so necessary - **that the sponsors likewise should be thrust into danger? Who both themselves, by reason of mortality, may fail to fulfil their promises, and may be disappointed by the development of an evil disposition,** in *those for whom they stood?* The Lord does indeed say, "Forbid them not to come unto me." Let them "come," then, while they are growing up; let them "come" while they are learning, while they are learning whither to come; let them become Christians when they have become able to know Christ. Why does the innocent period of life hasten to the "remission of sins?" More caution will be exercised in worldly matters: so that one who is not trusted with earthly substance is trusted with divine! Let them know how to "ask" for salvation, that you may seem (at least) to have given "to him that asketh." For no less cause must the unwedded also be deferred - in whom the ground of temptation is prepared, alike in such as never were wedded by means of their maturity, and in the widowed by means of their freedom - until they either marry, or else be more fully strengthened for continence. If any understand the weighty import of baptism, they will fear its reception more than its delay: sound faith is secure of salvation.[1]

Other authors could be cited as well; however, none of them ever insinuated that infant baptism was a "new" thing, or that it was contrary to the standard practice of the Church since the beginning. Indeed, if the Apostles did not practice infant baptism, then surely someone, somewhere, would have spoken up for the truth and set the record straight. They would have shown that the Apostles had never supported infant baptism as the norm for the Church. But no one ever said anything. We have no one who even hinted that infant baptism was wrong.

As we move on through Church history, we see the same thing in the next century. Pelagius, the early Church heretic, came under

---

[1] On Baptism. Chap. XVIII. - Of the Persons to Whom, and the Time When, Baptism Is to Be Administered.

fire for his heretical views of original sin. He believed that infants are born without the stain of sin on them; and thus, they are capable of living a perfect life in the same way that Adam was capable of it. Of course, Augustine wrote volumes of response, defending the essential doctrine of original sin. Within this great "debate," there are some stunning sayings from both parties. You see, Augustine and all orthodox Christians at the time were asking Pelagius and his followers this question: "If there is no original sin, then why baptize infants?" The popular view at the time was that baptism did not just wash away the sins you have committed, but also the original sin you inherited from Adam. The Pelagians, eager to be seen as orthodox in their views, were quick to point out that they *did, indeed, baptize infants.* The quotes below are taken from this debate.

Augustine says...

> Now, seeing that they (the Pelagians) admit the necessity of baptizing infants,—**finding themselves unable to contravene that authority of the universal Church, which has been unquestionably handed down by** the Lord and His apostles,—they cannot avoid the further concession, that infants require the same benefits of the Mediator, in order that, being washed by the sacrament and charity of the faithful, and thereby incorporated into the body of Christ, which is the Church, they may be reconciled to God, and so live in Him, and be saved, and delivered, and redeemed, and enlightened. But from what, if not from death, and the vices, and guilt, and thralldom, and darkness of sin? And, inasmuch as they do not commit any sin in the tender age of infancy by their actual transgression, original sin only is left.[1]

You see, Augustine concluded that because we know "unquestionably" that infant baptism came directly from "the Lord and His apostles," and because we know that infants have not sinned in and of themselves; then they must be baptized for original sin. I do not agree with Augustine in everything; I only quote him in order to show that he unequivocally believed that infant baptism was

---

[1] The Nicene and Post-Nicene Fathers Vol. 5 pg 30

Apostolic doctrine. As I said above, the early Church was more Jewish and covenantal in their thinking. However, by this time, the Church was mostly made up of Gentiles who didn't have the same covenantal views, but rather, more individualistic views. They brought that individualism to their theology. But also notice how Pelagius argues in this debate:

> *I have been* defamed by certain persons for refusing the sacrament of baptism to infants, and promising the kingdom of heaven irrespective of Christ's redemption. *I have* **never heard even an impious heretic say this about infants,** Who indeed is so unacquainted with Gospel lessons, as not only to attempt to make such an affirmation, but even to be able to lightly say it or even let it enter his thought? **And then who is so impious as to wish to exclude infants from the kingdom of heaven, by forbidding them to be baptized and to be born again in Christ?**[1]

Now, I must point out that regardless of your view on baptism, the important point here is that two of the most educated men of the Christian Church in the fourth century—one orthodox, and the other heretical—had no idea of any controversy about infant baptism that had ever taken place. If you read Augustine, you will see him quoting many times from the Fathers prior to him. He was perhaps the most learned man to come out of the fourth century AD, and yet he said that infant baptism was "unquestionably handed down by the Lord and His apostles." Why had Augustine never heard or read of the apparent shift that our Baptist brethren speak of? Even the heretic Pelagius (a very learned man himself) said that he had never even heard an "impious heretic" say that infants shouldn't be baptized. That is significant! The Baptist idea of some sort of sudden shift from Credobaptism to Paedobaptism seems absolutely inconceivable! Someone would certainly have spoken about it. So how is it that these two men never even *heard* of such a controversy?

---

[1] The Nicene and Post-Nicene Fathers Vol. 5 pg 243-244 From two separate citations by Augustine, italics are my addition to make sense of the statement after removing Augustine's remarks.

I tell you: it was because there was no such controversy. As Augustine stated, infant baptism was handed down "by the Lord and His apostles."

CONCLUSION

As we come to the conclusion of this study on baptism, I think it's only appropriate that we should spend a little time discussing the baptism of our Lord, as well as the baptisms that our Lord Himself performed.

THE BAPTISM OF OUR LORD JESUS

Why was Jesus baptized? It's a fair and common question which I hear all the time. There have been a myriad of answers; some good, some flat-out blasphemous. But one in particular merits a closer look.

Baptists are fond of saying that you must "follow the Lord in His baptism." But I don't think that's possible. His baptism was not the same as ours. It was performed in the same way, to be sure. He had John pour or sprinkle water on His body. But was it for the purpose of symbolically washing away sin? Of course not. Was it in obedience to a prophet of God, calling for all Israel to be baptized? Maybe, but not likely. We all recognize the significant fact that Jesus started out His life of ministry with His baptism. We also recognize that immediately upon His baptism, He was anointed with the Holy Spirit. Then He took the extraordinary step of going immediately from there into the wilderness, to fast and be tempted for forty days. This is also significant. These are all highly symbolic events; or rather, they are the fulfilments of highly symbolic events recorded in Scripture.

Notice how nicely the events of Jesus' baptism were symbolized by the High Priest of the Old Testament. The High Priest was the representative of the people before God. He represented all of Israel. He, too, had to be washed prior to his ministry. His ministry represented what Israel's ministry was supposed to be in the world: to be the world's representatives to God, and to bring the world under God's submission. That ministry started when the High Priest was *consecrated,* and that consecration started with *baptism.*

> And Aaron and his sons you shall bring to the door of the tabernacle of meeting, and you shall wash them with water (Ex. 29:4).

This was an administered baptism, not a self-washing. It was administered by Moses. And of course, you know what was standing there before the door of the tabernacle of meeting, don't you? The laver. Do you really picture Aaron sitting in the laver as if he was in a bathtub, with Moses scrubbing him down? It's quite a silly picture. Nothing but water was ever physically inside the laver.[1] This was a washing by effusion. Moses took water from the laver (which was the only source of water at the "door of the tabernacle"), and he poured it over Aaron. Then Moses was commanded to enrobe Aaron with the robes of his office, and then...

> And you shall take the anointing oil, pour it on his head, and anoint him. (Ex. 29:7)

Sound familiar yet? What happened immediately after Jesus' baptism? He was anointed by the Holy Spirit. Jesus, your High Priest, went through the exact same ceremony of consecration—He was baptized and anointed. I can see John the Baptizer putting Jesus' robes back on Him, as the Holy Spirit descended from above. Then, to cap it off, as the representative of Israel, Jesus immediately began to wander in the wilderness for forty days. This represented Israel's wandering in the wilderness for forty years.

---

[1] See section on The Laver.

The picture is astounding. And yet I have heard people try to respond to this by saying that our Lord did not become a Priest at the hands of men, or that He wasn't a Levitical priest...and so on. And while I agree whole-heartedly with the facts of the case—that Jesus was not a Levitical priest, and that He was not made a Priest by men; I also understand that the Levitical priesthood was a *typical priesthood*, and that it was a part of that tabernacle service which had its *reality* in heaven.

Now this is the main point of the things we are saying: **We have such a High Priest,** who is seated at the right hand of the throne of the Majesty in the heavens, **a Minister** of the sanctuary and **of the true tabernacle which the Lord erected, and not man.** For every high priest is appointed to offer both gifts and sacrifices. Therefore it is necessary that this One also have something to offer. For if He were on earth, He would not be a priest, since **there are priests who offer the gifts according to the law; who serve the copy and shadow of the heavenly things,** as Moses was divinely instructed when he was about to make the tabernacle. For He said, **"SEE THAT YOU MAKE ALL THINGS ACCORDING TO THE PATTERN SHOWN YOU ON THE MOUNTAIN** (Heb. 8:1-5).

Jesus' Priesthood was given to Him by God, not by John. Yet John was the *typical representative* of God, just as Moses was.[1] And it was God Himself Who anointed Jesus with the Holy Spirit at His baptism[2]; not in typology, but in reality.

The picture is too stark to ignore, and too plain to brush aside as a novelty. This one consecration of the High Priest in the Old Testament is distinctly recorded three times for us!

---

[1] "So he shall be your spokesman to the people. And he himself shall be as a mouth for you, and you shall be to him as God" (Ex. 4:16).

[2] "The word which God sent to the children of Israel, preaching peace through Jesus Christ—He is Lord of all—that word you know, which was proclaimed throughout all Judea, and began from Galilee after the baptism which John preached: how God anointed Jesus of Nazareth with the Holy Spirit and with power, who went about doing good and healing all who were oppressed by the devil, for God was with Him" (Acts 10:36-38).

Our Lord delights in explaining theology to us in pictures. The entire Old Testament (while literally true) is one big picture of theological truths. We are infantile in our understanding, and our gracious Heavenly Father has given us a picture book to help us understand.

The Baptisms of our Lord Jesus

Now the Baptized becomes the Great Baptizer. Our Lord Jesus is now endowed with all power from God the Father; and the very next thing we find Him doing is...baptizing. Yes, baptizing is the business of the Great Baptizer. This Baptizer uses both the Holy Spirit and fire for His baptismal element. Let's take a look at His promise of what He would do, and His method of doing it.

> **I indeed baptize you with water** unto repentance, but He who is coming after me is mightier than I, whose sandals I am not worthy to carry. **He will baptize you with the Holy Spirit and fire** (Matt. 3:11).

> **I indeed baptized you with water, but He will baptize you with the Holy Spirit"** (Mark 1:8).

> John answered, saying to all, "**I indeed baptize you with water**; but One mightier than I is coming, whose sandal strap I am not worthy to loose. **He will baptize you with the Holy Spirit and fire"** (Luke 3:16).

> I did not know Him, but **He who sent me to baptize with water** said to me, 'Upon whom you see the Spirit descending, and remaining on Him, **this is He who baptizes with the Holy Spirit'** (John 1:33).

> For **John truly baptized with water**, but **you shall be baptized with the Holy Spirit** not many days from now (Acts 1:5).

Then I remembered the word of the Lord, how He said, **'John indeed baptized with water,** but **you shall be baptized with the Holy Spirit'** (Acts 11:16).

Now, when the Word of God goes to such pains to make a connection between "baptism with water" and "baptism with the Holy Spirit," you would think that there would be no dispute that the two are parallel. It should be obvious to everyone that baptism with water is *a picture* of baptism with the Holy Spirit. The former represents the latter. Both the application of water and the application of the Holy Spirit have the same name: *baptism*. So if the Bible never directly tells us that "John poured out the water upon" someone, does that even matter when it *does* tell us emphatically that the Holy Spirit is "poured out" in baptism? I think not.

But you shall receive power when **the Holy Spirit has come upon you;** and you shall be witnesses to Me in Jerusalem, and in all Judea and Samaria, and to the end of the earth (Acts 1:8).

Therefore being exalted to the right hand of God, and having received from the Father the promise of **the Holy Spirit, He poured out this** which you now see and hear (Acts 2:33).

And as I began to speak, **the Holy Spirit fell upon them,** as upon us at the beginning (Acts 11:15).

AND IT SHALL COME TO PASS IN THE LAST DAYS, SAYS GOD, THAT **I WILL POUR OUT OF MY SPIRIT ON ALL FLESH;** YOUR SONS AND YOUR DAUGHTERS SHALL PROPHESY, YOUR YOUNG MEN SHALL SEE VISIONS, YOUR OLD MEN SHALL DREAM DREAMS (Acts 2:17).

While Peter was still speaking these words, **the Holy Spirit fell upon all those who heard the word.** And those of the circumcision who believed were astonished, as many as came with Peter, because **the gift of the Holy Spirit had been poured out** on the Gentiles also (Acts 10:44, 45).

I quote all of these, simply to show the stress that God has put upon this in His Word. Perhaps the immersionist should allow the Bible to tell him how something is to be done, instead of listening to fallible men.

But what about baptism with fire? It, too, is compared with water baptism; so what does that mean? Well, as I've explained, baptism with water is a purification. That is exactly what fire is as well. Fire is used in Scripture, not only to refer to hell, but also to represent a purging influence. Our Lord purifies us with the fire of suffering. The red heifer had to be burned outside the camp, just as our Lord had to suffer outside the camp.[1]

FINAL NOTE

My Paedobaptist brethren, I sincerely hope this study has been beneficial for you. It is my prayer that in some small way this book will help us to achieve unity amongst brethren. I know, it's wishful thinking. It seems that the norm is that division comes from discussing this topic. But for many of those who choose to divide over this issue, it is simply because they don't know what the Bible actually teaches, and just like me, they were following "the first to plead his cause" without allowing for the "neighbor" to come and examine his arguments. If this book at all helps even some of the Church of Jesus Christ work through this disagreement among brethren in a more biblical way, I will consider it a work well worth the labor. Our Credobaptist brethren are dearly beloved of our

---

[1] A note on Numbers 19, from George Bush, says: "In the present rite we may safely consider the burning of the heifer as representing the excruciating sufferings of Christ, its ashes the permanent merit of his sacrifice, the running or living water the power and grace of his Holy Spirit, called the water of life and the laver of regeneration, while the mixture of the two together fitly represents the inseparable union which exists between the justification and the sanctification of a sinner." George Bush, *Notes on Numbers* pg 272

Lord, and thus, they must equally be dearly beloved by us. But the Baptists have been on the attack for far too long with too little coming from the Paedobaptist camp, not enough "neighbors" are willing to engage them, and examine their doctrines critically. Now it's time to go on the offensive and contend earnestly for this doctrine which is a "foundation" of the faith ranked right up there with repentance and eternal judgement.[1]

And let me end with a word to my Credobaptist brethren who may have read this.

First of all, this was not written to you. If it were, it would have perhaps been worded differently. But please accept my sincere apologies if I have offended you in the way I have said anything in this book. It was certainly not my intention.

Secondly, I know that perhaps some of you are unconvinced and will still wish to argue about this or that detail, and I'm all for the discussion. Feel free to engage me with thoughtful arguments and I'll be happy to respond in kind. You are my Brother. My beloved Brother. And as your neighbour I'll be happy to examine your arguments. Only, don't be petty. I have given you arguments which I believe destroy the entire Baptist doctrine of Baptism right from the Bible. If I have missed a relevant passage or two, don't delude yourself into thinking that I "had no answer for it". I simply concentrated on the core arguments and much of the minutia, so forgive me if I have not covered every single relevant verse in the bible. Every time I pick up my Bible I find more to add to this, but I had to stop somewhere. This is not an exhaustive study as there are literally hundreds of books written on this topic. But I believe this study is thorough enough to come to the conclusion that the Baptist position is in grave error, and the Paedobaptist doctrine is on solid scriptural ground.

And lastly, there are also some of you who have been convinced, and now you are a Paedobaptist. I say praise the Lord Jesus! It means we have one less doctrine dividing us. So now engage your Baptist brethren with passion, but in love. When Augustine entered into a

---

[1] Hebrews 6:1-2

debate with the Manicheans, a cult[1] he himself had been a part of, he started off by saying,

> "Let those rage against you who have never been led astray in the same way that they see that you are... I can on no account rage against you; for ... I must be as patient towards you as my associates were with me"[2]

So remember, you yourself were once a Baptist in ignorance. So be patient with your brethren. Engage them by all means, but you were once there as well, so of all people you would know what they are going through.

NOW UNTO THE KING ETERNAL, IMMORTAL, INVISIBLE, THE ONLY WISE GOD, BE GLORY FOREVER AND EVER! AMEN.

---

[1] I am by no means saying that Baptists are in a "cult" I am only quoting Augustine's interaction with them as a show of brotherly patience for those that he left behind.

[2] Augustin, Against the Manicheans. Ch 2&3

Selected Bibliography[1]

Credobaptist perspective

Ball, G.H. *Christian Baptisms, the Duty, the Act and the Subjects.* Dover. Freewill Baptist Printing Establishment. 1860

Beasley-Murray, G.R. *Baptism in the New Testament.* London, Macmillan & Co Ltd, 1963

Carson, Alexander. *Baptism... It's Mode and Subjects.* Grand Rapids, MI. Kregel Publications, Reprint 1981

Crampton, W. Gary. *From Paedobaptism to Credobaptism.* Owensboro, KY. Reformed Baptist Academic Press, 2010

Culver, Robert Duncan. Systematic Theology. Great Britain. Christian Focus Publications Ltd. 2005

Ford, David B. *Studies on The Baptismal Question.* Boston, H.A. Young & Co., 1879

Gill, John. *Body of Divinity.* Atlanta GA. Turner Lassetter, Reprint 1965

Grudem, Wayne. *Systematic Theology.* Grand Rapids, MI. Zondervan, 1994

Hinton, Isaac Tayler. *History of Baptism.* Philadelphia PA. American Baptist Publication and S.S. Society. 1840

Howell, Robert Boyte C. *The Evils of Infant Baptism.* Richmond VA. Virginia Baptist S.S. and Publication Society. 1852

Jewett, Milo P. *The Mode and Subjects of Baptism.* Boston, MA. Gould, and Lincoln. 1854

Johnson, Jeffrey D. *The Fatal Flaw of the Theology Behind Infant Baptism.* Free Grace Press, 2010

Malone, Fred A. *The Baptism of Disciples Alone.* Cape Coral, FL. Founders Press, 2003

---

[1] This Bibliography does not include the numerous commentaries and bible dictionaries that were researched for this book.

Strong, A.H. *Systematic Theology*. Fleming H. Revell Company, Reprint 1960

Waldron, Samuel E. with Richard C. Barcellos. *A Reformed Baptist Manifesto*. Palmdale CA, Reformed Baptist Academic Press, 2004

Warns, Johannes. Baptism. *Studies in the Original Christian Baptism*. Minneapolis, MN. Klock & Klock, Reprint 1980

Paedobaptist perspective

Baird, Samuel J. *The Great Baptizer -A Bible History of Baptism*. Philadelphia PA. James H. Baird, 1882.

Beecher, Edward. *Baptism, with reference to it's Import and Modes*. New York, NY. John Wiley, 1849

Booth, Robert R. *Children of the Promise*. Phillipsburg, NJ. P&R Publishing, 1995

Dale, James W. *Classic Baptism*. Mundelein, IL. Bolchazy-Carducci Publishers, Inc. Reprint 2008

Dale, James W. *Judaic Baptism*. Wauconda, IL. Bolchazy-Carducci Publishers, Inc. Reprint 1991

Dale, James W. *Johannic Baptism*. Wauconda, IL. Bolchazy-Carducci Publishers, Inc. Reprint 1993

Dale, James W. *Christic Baptism and Patristic Baptism*. Wauconda, IL. Bolchazy-Carducci Publishers, Inc. Reprint 1995

Elliot, A.B. R. *Dipping not Baptizing, The Author's Opinion of the Subject, Mode, and Importance of Water-Baptism according to the Scriptures*. London. H. Trapp. 1787

Fairfield, Edmund B. *Letters on Baptism*. Wrightstown, NJ. American Presbyterian Press (Date unknown)

Gallaher, Thomas. *A Short Method with the Dipping Anti-Pedobaptists*. St. Louis, Presbyterian Publishing Company Print. 1878

Johnson, Thos. Cary. *Baptism in the Apostolic Age*. Richmond VA. Presbyterian Committee of Publication. 1912

Lathrop, Joseph. *Sermons on the Mode and Subjects of Christian Baptism*. Northampton. William Butler, 1803

Mackay, W. A. *Immersion & Immersionists*. American Presbyterian Press, Reprint (Date unknown)

Marcel, Peirre. *The Biblical Doctrine of Infant Baptism*. London, James Clarke & Co. Ltd. 1959

McMillian, E. *The Evils of Dr. Howell's book on the "Evils of Infant Baptism"*. New York, NY. M. W. Dodd. 1855

M'Crie, Thomas. *Lectures on Christian Baptism*. Edinburgh. Johnstone & Hunter, 1850.

Murray, John. Christian Baptism. Philadelphia, PA. Presbyterian and Reformed Publishing Company, 1962

Rayburn, Robert G. *What About Baptism?* Grand Rapids MI. Baker Books House, 1979.

Spencer, Duane E. *Holy Baptism*. Tyler, TX. Geneva Ministries, 1984

Stearns, J.G.D. *The Meaning and Power of Baptism*. New York, NY. N. Tibbals & Sons, Publishers. 1877

Wikner, Benjamin K. *To You and Your Children*. Moscow, ID. Canon Press, 2005

Index of Scripture Texts

Mark

1:4—34,35,55
1:5—55
1:8—55,195
5:22, 23, 41,
  42—111
7:3—152
7:3, 4—74
7:4—32,36,152
7:8—32
9:17-27—111
10:13-16—112
16:16—21,22,
  36

Luke

1:41, 44—99
2:12, 16—99
3:4-6—42
3:16—195
4:10—157
4:27—151
6:40—130
7:29, 30—37
11:37, 38—152
11:37-39—37
11:38—32,74
18:15—23,99
18:15, 16—
  97,112
18:15-17—
  98,100,102
24:44-46—70

John

1:19-25—75
1:25—74
1:33—195
2:18-22—70
3—38
3:22-27—64
3:23—168
3:25—33,151
4:7—141
4:10—79
4:13, 14—79
4:39-42—44
4:46-54—111
6:66—25,132
7:37-39—79
8:5—100
11:55—144
15:2-6—164
15:5—52
15:26—81
17:6—28

Acts

1:4-5—83
1:5—195
1:8—196
2:1,2,14-18—
  83
2:17—196
2:33—196
7:19—99
7:38—66,106
8—44
8:9, 10—43
9:1—131

9:19—131
10:36-38—194
10:44, 45—196
10:44-48—84
11:15—196
11:15,16—84
11:16—196
11:26—131
13:48—163
15:10—131
17:11—6
20:7—131
22:22—100

Romans

2:20—129
4:11—108
5:15—12
6:3, 4—47
6:4—51
8:15,23—105
9:4—105
10:18—42
11:17, 18—107
15:4—6
15:15—12

1 Corinthians

1:16—116
7:14—92
10—29
10:1—122
10:1, 2—121
15:3, 4—70
15:4—73
15:22—12